Perceptions of Justice

Law, Literature, and Film

Terry Lewis

ISBN: 979-8-9989266-2-4

Library of Congress LCCN: 2026914134

Cover art by Bill Day

Interior design by Draft Works

Barry Books
Rockville, Maryland

terrylewisbooks.com
www.the-justice-institute.org

Dedication

In memory of

Barry Schaller and Ken Henley

Table of Contents

Acknowledgement

My heartfelt thanks go to the many people who read a draft of this book, some in the early stages and some at the end. Their observations, comments, and suggestions were very helpful. They are: Fran Lewis, Liz Jameson, Lisa Blackwell, Marina Brown, Sam Staley, Claire Staley, Harry Anstead, Major Harding, Phil Padovano, George Reynolds, Tom Bateman, Patsy Palmer, Marjorie Turnbull, and Rob McNeely.

1

Introduction

"Injustice anywhere is a threat to justice everywhere."

—*Martin Luther King*

"There is no such thing as justice - in or out of court."

—*Clarence Darrow*

"We may try to see things as objectively as we please. Nonetheless, we can never see them with any eyes except our own."

—*Benjamin N. Cardozo*

LET'S START WITH two images: One from the O.J. Simpson case and one from an Ally Bank commercial. The trial of O.J. Simpson for the murder of his wife and a friend was carried live on television, gavel to gavel, to a large audience. When the verdict was read aloud, the cameras caught the reaction of two different groups. Those outside the courthouse, composed mostly of minorities, applauded and gave out shouts of joy. In contrast, those in the mostly white crowd at a Brentwood coffee shop were shocked, dismayed, and disgusted, convinced that an obvious killer had escaped justice.

In an Ally Bank television commercial a few years back, a little girl is asked by a man if she'd like a pony. She nods and says yes, and the man gives her a toy pony, a stuffed animal. The man asks a second little girl in the room if she'd like a pony and the girl says yes. The man then brings in a live, small pony and gives it to her. The second girl is delighted, but the hurt and disappointment on the first girl's face tells it all. She says, "You didn't say I could have a real pony." To which the man replies, "You didn't ask."

The Ally Bank commercial highlights the point that even a small child understands the concept of fairness. The reaction to the O. J. verdict dramatically illustrates how reasonable people of good faith can view the same result and have completely different perceptions of whether it was just. Both are important premises for this book.

What is this elusive concept we call justice? Is it, like beauty, in the eye of the beholder? Is it, as Justice Potter Stewart suggested about pornography, difficult to define but we know it when we see it? Are there objective criteria we can apply, and if so, what are they? How do we balance competing values in deciding what is just or fair in a given situation? For example, what is more important, a fair result or a fair process? What affects our analysis and why? Why is it that people might come to opposite conclusions as to whether justice was done in a particular situation? Are there ways to reconcile our differing perceptions of justice? These are some of the questions readers will be asked to ponder in this volume.

Maybe you agree with Clarence Darrow's cynical quote above, that there is no such thing as justice, in or out of court, or that justice may exist as a concept, but it can never be achieved. And maybe you are right. But I hope you will agree that seeking justice is worth the effort, that it is valuable even if the goal remains elusive.

In 1997, my first novel was published. With no expertise other than my status as a published author, I was asked to develop and teach a course on law and literature for Florida judges. Eventually, I came up with a title, *Perceptions of Justice*, and expanded the scope to include film and essays, as well as works of fiction. An underlying theme of the course was that a ruling should not only be legally correct, it should also be perceived as just in order to promote confidence in the fairness of the process.

I helped teach this course several times over the years until my retirement from the bench in 2019. In the back of my mind, I thought perhaps to one day put down on paper some general thoughts and observations on the subject, not just for judges, but for anyone who values fairness and justice. My experience in teaching a version of the course to laypersons for OLLI (Osher Life Long Learning Institute) reinforced the notion in my mind.

Justice is not the exclusive province of those who write the laws, or those who enforce them, or apply them to resolve disputes. It is not a subject only for philosophers or academics. We all have a stake in it. And most of us have a strong, innate sense of justice, of what is fair. It is directly tied to our notion of morality, of what is right and what is wrong, about how we should treat other people and how we expect to be treated. A shared moral code, a shared sense of justice, is the glue that holds a society together.

Moreover, our innate sense of justice and fairness has a much broader application than just the courts or the "justice system." Demands for racial, economic, social, environmental, and other forms of justice are pervasive in political discourse. Nearly every question of public policy can be productively analyzed and debated in terms of what is fair and just. Although I will focus primarily on the judicial branch of government in this volume, the principles and values underpinning our concept of justice are equally applicable to the executive and legislative branches. An understanding of how we view such concepts is thus a helpful tool for every citizen of our democratic republic.

This book is not intended to be the kind of scholarly work that appears in university publications or law reviews. There will be no citations to authorities or studies or surveys, and no footnotes. I will share a little about my background and my views on the subject. I will also recount some of my experiences as a judge and some of the cases I handled in order to put a practical face on what may seem like an academic, esoteric subject. And perhaps it will demystify the law and the legal process a bit for those of you who do not labor in the trenches of this field. But the primary intent is to promote introspection on the part of you, the reader, for you to understand the what and the why of your perception of justice, of what is fair, and to understand why others may differ.

To do this we will use actual court cases, essays, works of fiction, and references to scenes from films as springboards for discussion. I like using works of fiction and film because the stories we tell each other both reflect and affect how we think about justice. It is not necessary that you watch the movies or read the works of fiction, essays and appellate opinions that are referenced, though it wouldn't hurt if you did.

I must admit that I approached this project with a bit of trepidation. Who am I to pontificate on such a topic? Do I have any particular insight into the subject? More wisdom than others? No. The subject has occupied the minds of some of the greatest philosophers in recorded history and filled the pages of countless volumes. Could I really imagine that reflections on my experiences or my take on justice would be of interest to anybody else? It takes a hint of vanity on the part of the author to presume so. And it gave me pause, for sure.

Indeed, I wrote the first draft quickly in 2019, then I put it aside. But I decided to take it back up and finish it, figuring that the exercise itself would be worthwhile. I hope, of course, that you will agree.

II

Law, Justice, and Morality: Foundations

Blessed are they who maintain justice, who constantly do what is right.

—*Psalm 106:3*

At his best, man is the noblest of all animals; separated from law and justice he is the worst.

—*Aristotle*

Defining Justice

REACHING A CONSENSUS on a definition of justice is probably not that difficult. The following is what you might find in a dictionary: Justice - 1. Moral rightness; equity. 2. Honor; fairness. 3. Good reason. 4. Fair handling; due reward or treatment. 5. The administration and procedure of law.

These definitions of justice seem reasonable in different contexts. Fair handling and due reward or treatment is perhaps the most common understanding, and has the broadest application, in and out of court. We generally associate the term justice with the application and adherence to established laws, rules, and principles. The term conjures up images of trials and court cases, of sentencings and appellate rulings. We generally think of fairness as less formal, with broader application, encompassing the moral or ethical precept of treating others without bias or favoritism. They are not quite synonymous, perhaps, but for our purposes it is helpful to think of them as interchangeable.

Agreeing on a workable definition of justice as fair handling and due reward or punishment may not be difficult, at least in the abstract. But reaching a consensus on what that looks like in each situation often proves more difficult. Is there a prism through which we can view actions, a framework with which we can analyze any situation, to give us a consistent answer to what is just?

Over the centuries, great thinkers and philosophers have devoted considerable time and effort to the subject of justice, and perhaps this is a good place to start. I mean, why try to re-invent the wheel? It would be comforting if we could find a perfect fit, an organized way of looking at the subject that makes sense, and a set of principles that unerringly apply.

Some Historical and Philosophical Concepts of Justice

It is beyond the scope of this volume, and my very limited expertise, to provide a thorough exploration of the numerous schools of thought on the subject of justice. Nor, I suspect, would you want to wade through it. I offer only a short summary of some of the more common ones and give you my take on each.

The notion of justice or fairness is, at its heart, one of political philosophy. It is part of the answer to the question: How should we conduct ourselves and what should we expect of others? It is also a matter of ethics or morality. Being fair and just is considered to be a virtue. So, let's take a look at some of those ideas. And my apologies to the real philosophers.

Justice as Rendering Each His Due Punishment or Reward

Immanuel Kant (1724-1804) was an influential German philosopher who wrote on several topics, including justice. Kant's "categorical imperative" requires that all people act in a morally correct manner at all times, specifically, to avoid causing harm or inflicting damage upon another person. In this regard, Kant defines an act as 'morally correct' if it can be applied as a universal law.

According to Kant, those who violate the rules we all share gain an unfair advantage over those who do not. Punishment is used as a means to restore the balance between the law-abiding citizens and the criminals, removing any unfairly gained advantage from the criminals. He saw justice as a balancing of the scales, an eye-for-an-eye approach.

Interestingly, the idea that a function of punishment is deterrence, both for the individual and for the general public, was rejected by Kant. His theory of justice was premised on the proposition that every person deserves to be treated as an end in himself, and not a means to some other end. We have no business, he would argue, punishing someone as a means to deter others. The only consideration is to determine what punishment is necessary to balance the scales, to bring things back to an equilibrium.

This eye-for-an-eye, retributive theory is very popular, and at the core of most formal legal codes. It runs deep in our culture. Consider this observation by the U.S. Supreme Court:

The instinct for retribution is part of the nature of man, and channeling that instinct in the administration of criminal justice serves an important purpose in promoting the stability of a society governed by law. When people begin to believe that organized society is unwilling or unable to impose upon criminal offenders the punishment they 'deserve,' then there are sown the seeds of anarchy—of self-help, vigilante justice, and lynch law. Gregg v. Georgia 428 U.S. 153-241 (1976).

Consider this passage from an editorial in the Tallahassee Democrat on September 12, 2001, the day after terrorist attacks on the twin towers and the pentagon:

"Justice, justice, shall you pursue," reads Deuteronomy, part of the sacred text of both Jews and Christians. It is not simply a strong suggestion. It's a command. The Quran calls justice "an unassailable fortress, built on the brow of a mountain which cannot be overthrown." Our Constitution was written to ensure justice. Not encourage. Ensure.

The civilized world's response to Tuesday's unspeakable horrors must be systematic, determined, and enduring. It need not be bloodthirsty revenge, but we must proceed with unusual vigor, and without remorse. This most certainly is not a war against any religion or group of people. The sobering realty, however, is that this is war. When the mass murderers and those who harbor them are identified – and they will be – they must be treated like war criminals...

There should be no qualms about how we respond. Justice, and our sense of humanity, demand it.

What do you think the editorial board was thinking justice would look like? Despite protestations to the contrary in the editorial, I suspect many readers, and the editorial board, saw bloodthirsty revenge as a very appropriate response to the terrorists' acts of the preceding day. What eventually happened to Osama Bin Laden? Certainly, most readers of this editorial envisioned some kind of punishment, differing only as to the nature and degree.

There is much to like about Kant's theory of justice, requiring that we act so as not to cause harm to others, that the laws should apply to everyone equally, that we should try to take away the advantage obtain by breaking those laws, balancing the scales so to speak, and that punishment should be premised on the dignity and worth of each individual. It's a helpful framework and as noted, most criminal codes are based on a retributive theory of justice. I find, however, that I cannot go all the way with Kant. There are too many unanswered questions.

First, how do we know what punishment a person deserves? For example, Kant argues that death is the only appropriate punishment for murder. Nothing else will balance the scales.

But all murders are not the same. Florida law makes a distinction between a planned, or premeditated, intentional killing and one done without premeditation, but under circumstances that suggest a callous disregard for whether death results. The first is murder in the first degree and punishable by death, or life in prison, as a jury decides. The other is called second degree murder and is punishable by up to life in prison. Death is not an option.

Manslaughter is another crime that involves the unjustified killing of another person but without premeditation or a callous disregard for life. Examples would include a bar fight in which you hit a person but didn't intend to kill them, or you drove while intoxicated, got into an accident and killed someone. The punishment prescribed for manslaughter is less than that for second degree murder.

Even with first degree, premeditated murder, there are aggravating and mitigating factors. A person who carefully plans a murder, who carries it out with extreme cruelty, with physical and psychological torture, is different than a person who, in the heat of passion, kills someone who has just raped his wife. Under the law, both are guilty of first degree, premeditated murder. But most of you, I think, would spare the man who killed his wife's attacker from the death penalty. Some of you might argue for a much-reduced sentence, or even no penalty at all.

There will also be aggravating and mitigating factors in crimes other than murder, as well. Can we all agree on what a defendant deserves in these cases? Kant would argue that universal agreement is not required, only that the authority imposing the punishment do so consistent with the retributive theory of giving the defendant what he deserves. Okay, but that means two defendants, similarly situated and under similar circumstances, convicted of the same crime, may receive very different punishments depending of which judge imposes sentence. Is that fair? Shouldn't we be striving for consistency across the board? Indeed, Florida's sentencing guidelines are an attempt to do just that.

I also believe that deterrence, both for the individual defendant and for the general public, is an appropriate consideration in determining a just punishment. One of the goals of punishment under Florida's sentencing code is deterrence. There is societal value in people understanding that wrongful conduct has consequences, as it may deter them from such conduct. And that value remains regardless of whether a particular defendant "deserves" the punishment imposed or whether it is necessary to deter that particular defendant. You are sending a message to the rest of the community.

Finally, if we are to respect each individual as an end in himself, should we not fashion a punishment that respects his individuality? If we focus solely on the nature of the crime and ignore the particulars of each defendant, are the scales really balanced? Do we not consider previous criminal conduct? An existing support system for a defendant that makes re-offending less likely? Yes, the punishment should fit the crime, but it should also fit the defendant.

I think most people expect something a little more nuanced, a consideration of a number of variables in determining what is an appropriate punishment in a particular case, for a particular defendant. So, as appealing as it might be in some respects, the Kantian approach is a little too rigid in my opinion.

I do, however, embrace the notion that respect for the individual requires us to hold him responsible for his conduct, just as it imposes on him the obligation to take responsibility for his actions. This is something not always appreciated by defendants. I recall one case in which I explained to the defendant that it was respect for him that compelled me to hold him responsible for his conduct and impose a lengthy sentence. He responded that he would rather have a little less respect, if it was all right with me, and a reduced sentence.

Plato offers another argument against Kant's strict retributive theory of punishment, at least as to the death penalty. Whereas Kant would say the only way to balance the scales for murder is to execute the murderer, Plato would argue that there is no justice in harming a human being, regardless of the person's conduct. The premise, I suppose, is that two wrongs do not make a right, that we should, as a people, be better than the outliers who act outside the moral sphere. This is consistent with Ghandi's observation that an eye for an eye and soon everyone is blind. This sounds good and noble, and you may convince some people to reject the death penalty on this basis, but I think the desire to punish is too strong in our national psyche for it to have wider application.

Just Government and Property

For James Madison, one of our founding fathers and primary architect of our constitution, justice was directly related to private property rights. He argued that our right to be treated fairly, and to have our liberty respected by others, was based on the concept of property. Just as we have a property right in land and physical possessions, we have a property right in our person, our liberty, our means of livelihood, even in our opinions. And government, Madison argued, is instituted to protect property of every sort. Thus, a just government is one which impartially secures to every person those property rights.

This seems like a helpful way to look at the big picture, to justify our individual right to justice, but it doesn't really answer the central question of what justice is, and how we know it has been achieved in a given situation. We take away people's property and their liberty all the time, and in the name of justice. How do we know that this deprivation is, in fact, just? So, while the concept of having a property right in liberty might be an acceptable place to start, it doesn't get us to the finish line.

Justice and Utility

The "utilitarian approach" uses a simple formula—whatever is best for the most people is the fair and just course of action. It is of general utility and social usefulness for people to have certain rights and obligations, and that those rights be protected and the obligations enforced by all of us. It is in our mutual self-interest to do so.

This is not a bad approach and will work fine in many situations, but it only holds up, in my opinion, if it embraces a fairly broad idea of what is of general utility and social usefulness. Who decides what is best for the most people? And there may be some things that have an intangible value but no specific utility, things that are good only for a very limited number of people, but worth having for the long-term benefit of everyone. The real danger with this theory is that it may lead to a tyranny of the majority, or of those who decide what is best for the most.

Justice as Part of the Social Contract

The social contract theory posits that individuals have consented, either explicitly or tacitly, to surrender some of their freedoms and submit to the authority of the ruler or to the decision of a majority in exchange for protection of their remaining rights and maintenance of the social order. The term takes its name from *The Social Contract*, a 1762 book by Jean-Jacques Rousseau that discussed this concept. Prominent 17th- and 18th-century theorists of social contract and natural rights include Thomas Hobbes, John Locke, and our friend, Immanuel Kant.

Thomas Hobbes famously wrote in Leviathan (1651) that in a "state of nature," human life would be "solitary, poor, nasty, brutish and short." In the absence of political order and law, everyone would have unlimited natural freedoms, including the "right to all things" and thus the freedom to plunder, rape and murder; there would be an endless "war of all against all." To avoid this, free men contract with each other to establish political community (civil society) in which they all gain security in return for subjecting themselves to an absolute sovereign, one man or an assembly of men. Hobbes saw absolute government as the only alternative to the terrifying anarchy of a state of nature.

Locke had a more positive view of human nature, seeing people in a state of nature as basically good, but seeking to gain civil rights in return for accepting the obligation to respect and defend the rights of others. Everyone voluntarily gives up some freedoms for the benefit of mutual protection of the remaining ones.

Locke also argued that all people have natural, God-given rights that no government is entitled to take away. When the government fails to secure their natural rights, citizens can withdraw their obligation to obey, or change the leadership through elections or other means, including, when necessary, violence. Sound familiar? You'll find these concepts invoked in the Declaration of Independence.

I like to think of myself as an optimist. But I am also fond of the saying, "Hope for the best, plan for the worst." So, I have to go with Hobbes over Locke on the underlying basis for the social contract theory. The implicit social contract is more likely based on mutual distrust and mutual coercion. So long as it seems to work for enough people to continue the buy-in, it works.

The social contract theory is sort of like the free-market approach to law and justice—what rights are you willing to give up to have more security for the remaining rights? Supply and demand. It's also consistent with Madison's concept of property rights being the basis for the protection of our liberty. Of course, as Benjamin Franklin purportedly observed, "Those who would give up essential liberty to purchase a little temporary safety, deserve neither liberty nor safety."

So, the theory doesn't tell us whether the terms of this social contract are fair, nor what would be a just result when the terms are violated. It does, however, offer a roadmap to guide us toward an answer. If we start at the intersection of natural law and positive (man-made) law, we can at least judge whether a given law is consistent with what we see as fundamental rights.

Justice as Rule-Following

There are some who would say that if it is the legally correct result, it is a just result. There is bound to be too much disagreement to make justice perfect in practice, so the best we can do is follow the laws and rules validly enacted.

This is a little too rigid for my taste, too much like lemmings blindly, unquestioningly, following each other over a cliff, or the ostrich head in the sand approach. It ignores the fact that a legal and fair process does not always produce a fair and just result, at least in the minds of objective observers. It is why laws get changed in many cases.

Justice as Rules Imposed by the Powerful (Might Makes Right)

Some argue that justice is what those in power say it is. They enact laws with a view to their own advantage but proclaim that they are for the public good. This is a cynical view, and it may be correct in the final analysis. It is similar to the observation that history is written by the victors. Even in a democracy, those in power write the rules, and they almost always favor those who write them, and often at the expense of the powerless.

Power is retained by manipulating the general public into believing those in power act on behalf of the common good. It is frustrating sometimes to see how easy it is. Now, many of those in power are genuinely convinced that they are, in fact, acting from altruistic intentions. But the fact is, their idea of the common good is almost never at odds with what is of benefit to them.

A subset of this concept would be critical race theory. CRT scholars argue that the social and legal construction of race advances the interests of white people at the expense of people of color, and that the liberal notion of "neutral" laws is a fallacy. Rather, it allows those in power to justify racially discriminatory outcomes. It is institutional racism at work as opposed to individual biases and prejudices. One could argue that the recent efforts to ban the teaching of CRT and vilify it as anti-American tends to make its point. What are those in power so afraid of?

As we will explore later, the subjective perception of justice is arguably just as important, perhaps more so, than achieving the objective just result. And it is important to recognize and address how a given result might be perceived by different groups in developing a just society. While this cynical view might indeed be the political reality, I would not call it justice.

So, where does that leave us if none of these philosophical approaches give us the complete answer to determining what is fair and just? Perhaps you find some of the precepts helpful. Are there principles or values, components in our concept of justice, that are important to us in evaluating whether justice was done? If so, how do we weigh and balance competing principles and values? Where do our priorities lie? Our next section will explore answers to these questions by using works of fiction and film, essays and actual court cases that present themes of law, justice, and morality.

III

Law, Justice, and Morality: Principles, Values, and Components

Whenever a separation is made between liberty and justice, neither, in my opinion, is safe.

—*Edmund Burke*

Extremism in the defense of liberty is no vice. And moderation in the pursuit of justice is no virtue.

—*Barry Goldwater*

LET'S START WITH a little experiment, a self-evaluation relative to what I suggest is a core component in our concept of justice.

Ends versus Means

Do the ends justify the means? Or are the means the end? In other words, what is more important, a fair result or a fair process? Your answer to this says a lot about your concept of justice. More precisely, where you are on the ends versus means continuum is a very important factor in how you decide if justice is done in a specific situation. It is also where we will find the most disagreement among us as to what is just.

I think most of us can agree that the less tension between a fair procedure and just result, the better. Where there is tension, however, some of us are more willing to look the other way when an affected person disregards fair process in favor of a "just" result—and even applaud it, depending on the situation. The closer we are to the situation, the more personal it is to us, the more concerned we are with getting what we think is the fair and just result and less about how we get there.

Others have a higher threshold in this regard, at least when they are not directly affected. They are more appreciative of the value of an agreed-upon process to resolve disputes and determine what is just. They are willing to accept what may seem to be an unjust result, understanding that reasonable people can disagree, and appreciating the danger of arbitrariness when the agreed-upon process is ignored.

But even those who lean heavily toward fair process are willing to ignore the rules when the stakes are too high, the danger too real, and the consequences so dire. It's what I like to call the *Dirty Harry* scenario. A child is locked in a box with maybe thirty minutes of air left and Harry confronts the person who admits what he has done but won't tell Harry where the child is. "I want a lawyer," the man says. Harry shoots him in the knee and the man tells him where the child is.

What do you think? Where are you on the ends versus means continuum? Let's try a little exercise.

With which of the following statements do you most agree?

A. The ends justify the means. A just result is more important than a fair process.

B. The means are the end. A fair process is more important than a just result.

Think about it for a bit and choose one, commit to one of these. Go ahead. I'll wait.

Okay, I know some of you didn't do as instructed. And I'm disappointed. This is supposed to be interactive and an opportunity for introspection. So, if you didn't, you get another chance. Go ahead.

Now, I also understand that most of us are uncomfortable with an all-or-nothing approach to this question. Most of us probably think we are somewhere in between. So, okay, plot yourself on the scale below.

A————————————————————————B

I think it is helpful, and interesting, to examine where we place ourselves, and why, and to test our initial self-evaluation with concrete examples. It should give you some insight as to your philosophy of justice. Let's dig a little deeper with some fictional and real-life examples. Maybe, upon reflection, you might move yourself more one way or the other on the scale.

The Godfather

"For Justice, we must go to Don Corleone."

One of my favorites film clips to jumpstart a discussion on justice is the opening scene from *The Godfather. The Godfather* and *Godfather II* are two of my favorite movies—nobody likes GFIII.

I can't capture in print here the genius of the director's vision, the nuances created by setting and lighting, the tone of voice, the facial expressions and body language. There is no substitute for the clip itself, which is why I like to use it. Nevertheless, I will try to recreate the general impression, and quote some of the key dialogue.

It is the wedding day of the daughter of Don Corleone (the Godfather) and Sicilian tradition holds that the godfather grants favors on this day to those who ask. One such person is the local undertaker. As the movie begins, you hear the theme music playing softly in the background. The screen is black when you first hear the undertaker, whose name is Bonasera, speaking.

I believe in America. America has made my fortune. And I raised my daughter in the American fashion. I gave her freedom, but I taught her never to dishonor her family.

Gradually, as the man tells his story, the camera finds his face and then, more gradually, we see Don Corleone, sitting behind his desk, stroking a cat in his lap as he listens. Some other men stand nearby in the darkened room.

Bonasera tells the Don that two boys took his daughter for a drive, made her drink whiskey, then "tried to take advantage of her." When she resisted, "they beat her, like an animal…. *her nose was a'broken. Her jaw was a'shattered, held together by wire….*

Bonasera breaks down. The Don gestures for one of the men to give him a drink. Bonasera, taking the drink, sips from the shot glass.

I went to the police, like a good American. These two boys were brought to trial. The judge sentenced them to three years in prison—suspended sentence. Suspended sentence! They went free that very day! I stood in the courtroom like a fool. And those two bastards, they smiled at me. Then I said to my wife, for justice, we must go to Don Corleone.

When Vito Corleone asks him what he wants him to do, Bonasera whispers his request into the Don's ear.

That I cannot do, the Don says.

I'll give you anything you ask, the undertaker replies.

The Don is obviously disappointed. He points out that even though they've known each other for years, that his wife is godmother to the man's only child, *this is the first time you came to me for counsel, for help. I can't remember the last time that you invited me to your house for a cup of coffee.*

The undertaker says he didn't want to get in trouble.

Vito responds: *I understand. You found paradise in America, had a good trade, made a good living. The police protected you; and there were courts of law. And you didn't need a friend like me. But now you come to me and you say "Don Corleone give me justice." But you don't ask with respect. You don't offer friendship. You don't even think to call me Godfather. Instead, you come into my house on the day my daughter is to be married, and you ask me to do murder, for money.*

I ask you for justice.

That is not justice; your daughter is still alive.

Then they can suffer, as she suffers? He hesitates, then, *How much shall I pay you?*

The Don stands, turning his back toward him. *Bonasera... Bonasera... What have I ever done to make you treat me so disrespectfully? Had you come to me in friendship, then this scum that ruined your daughter would be suffering this very day. And that by chance if an honest man such as yourself should make enemies, then they would become my enemies. And then they would fear you.*

Bonasera bows his head. *Be my friend—Godfather?*

The Don shrugs and holds out his hand, palm down. After Bonasera kisses his hand, the Godfather says, *Good.* Then the Don utters one of the most famous lines in the movie, nay, in film history: *Someday, and that day may never come, I'll call upon you to do a service for me. But until that day, accept this justice as a gift on my daughter's wedding day.*

So, at this point, I want you to put this book down or stop the audio. Go get a piece of paper and a pen or pencil, or get on your laptop, and make a list of all the concepts related to justice you find in this scene. Then come back and we'll discuss it. If you are driving, let a passenger do it, or just do it in your head.

No, no. No cheating. I'm trying to make this interactive. I want you to discover what you think, not my take on it. Now go. I'll wait.

Well, for those of you who made a list, good for you. For the rest of you, well, that's okay. At least you're still with me. At any rate, let's compare notes.

Respect. Probably the key thing I take away from this scene is the importance of respect as a component of justice, or at least one's perception of whether they have received justice. The undertaker has been disrespected, by the boys, and by the system that did not impose sufficient punishment. "Suspended sentence! They went free that very day! I stood in the courtroom like a fool. And those two bastards, they smiled at me." The godfather in turn feels that he has been disrespected by the undertaker, who asks him "to do murder, for money."

It is a fundamental cornerstone of any organized society. People need to feel respected. They desire respect. If they can, they demand it. The feeling of being disrespected is what starts bar fights, gets people killed, makes people feel frustrated, angry, and powerless. It engenders distrust and lack of confidence in the political system that fails to show them the respect they feel they deserve.

You can see this play out every day and at every level. As I write this, under the rationalization of cutting waste, fraud, and abuse, thousands of federal workers have been fired with no notice and no opportunity to be heard. Perhaps you agree that there probably is some waste, some fat, even fraud in an organization as large as the federal government, and you are in favor of cutting it.

But put yourself in the shoes of those workers. How would you feel? Disrespected? Humiliated? Stigmatized by a blanket accusation that you know does not apply to you? Indeed, you were doing exactly what you were hired to do and receiving glowing appraisals of your work. Apply the Golden Rule to this situation. These firings may or may not have been lawful, but in the eyes of many, they sure weren't fair. And it sure doesn't engender trust and confidence in the political system.

Revenge. I suspect that revenge as justice is one of the most common themes in film. There are literally thousands of examples. It is such a visceral, primal reaction, it seems to be ingrained in our collective psyche. It has been observed that, "The urge to punish comes first. Reasons and attempted justification come later." (Soloman – *What is Justice?*)

We have a more polite term we use—retribution—but it's really revenge, dressed up. The third listed meaning of retribution in *Meriam-Webster* is: "something given or exacted in recompense *especially* : PUNISHMENT." One of its synonyms is revenge. With its prefix *re-*, meaning "back", *retribution* means literally "payback".

So, why do we shy away from acknowledging this truth? Why do we protest and say, that's not justice, that's revenge? One distinction, I suppose, is that we think of revenge as being more personal, an informal, outside-the-law punishment meted out by the victim of a crime or the victim's family, while retribution is something meted out by the collective group, the government, or some authoritative power.

God takes "divine retribution" on humans several times in the Old Testament, especially in the great flood that wipes out almost the entire human race. Retribution for criminal acts, usually in the form of a prison sentence, is taken by the state, not the victims. Either way, though, it is, indeed, payback, whether it's retribution for an insult in a high-school corridor or retribution for a guerrilla attack on a government building. The revenge in *The Godfather* scene is more like retribution than revenge, as it is a punishment exacted by an authority figure on ones who have violated a code.

Ineffectiveness of courts and the need for self-help. The theme of revenge or retribution goes hand in hand with two other common themes present in this scene from *The Godfather*: ineffectiveness of courts to obtain justice and the corresponding need for self-help. If we don't impose an appropriate punishment, we run the risk that people who are wronged will lose confidence that the "system" will give them justice. You may recall the earlier quote from the Supreme Court to the effect that, "When people begin to believe that organized society is unwilling or unable to impose upon criminal offenders the punishment they "deserve," then there are sown the seeds of anarchy—of self-help, vigilante justice, and lynch law." *Gregg v. Georgia* 428 U.S. 153, 241 (1976).

Sometimes, it is simply the courts following the law. For example, when a judge suppresses evidence obtained in violation of the Fourth Amendment, detractors lament that the defendant got off on a "technicality." Those seeking revenge do not much care about due process (a fair procedure.) Due process just gets in the way. That's why the villain often gets killed in the end. No muss, no fuss, no silly trial.

Physical violence as an acceptable tool for justice. The Don's authority, the reason Bonasera comes to him for justice, is self-realized from his willingness to use violence as a means to an end. His sense of justice, the private code he enforces, is backed up by brute force. He assures the undertaker that if he shows the proper respect and comes within his circle of protection, his enemies will become the Don's enemies. "And then they will fear you."

Some see this last point as a useful principle or guide for U.S. foreign policy, a fundamental basis for forming alliances, and I can see that. Justice in the international sense is often a matter of might makes right, buttressed by adherence to some vague code of conduct. But it clearly plays out on the "local" level as well. Those with power, willing to use harsh measures where needed, are the arbitrators of disputes, the enforcers of a private code of conduct that often mirrors the public one. The difference is in enforcement.

If made formal, this would be an example of a king, a dictator, or some kind of authoritarian ruler. Don Corleone decides what is fair, what is just. And in this world, and under this code, physical violence is an acceptable tool for justice. If you agree with him, everything is fine. If you don't, too bad. It is his might that makes it right.

So, as to ends vs means, there is no question where the undertaker falls. The father was not concerned with a fair process for the boys who assaulted his daughter. What had that gotten him? Disrespect and humiliation, but not justice. "For justice," he tells his wife, "we must go to Don Corleone." His idea of justice required a certain result. And neither he nor the godfather had a problem using violence to obtain that "just" result.

Proportionality. Some of you no doubt nodded your heads, at least figuratively, when Don Corleone responded to Bonasera's request that he grant him justice by killing the offenders. "That is not justice. Your daughter is still alive." It is inherent in the idea that the punishment should fit the crime. We understand that it's an eye for an eye, not two eyes for one eye—though some people may favor, as good policy, an overwhelming response, as it will tend to better deter future offenses.

Reciprocation/Loyalty. We also understand the idea that one is obligated to pay back the person who gives you a benefit. This is a quasi-contract, a fundamental building block for an organized society. In this instance, the Don is not interested in money for services, but rather that the undertaker understands that he is in his debt, and that debt is to be collected at a time and in a manner the Don chooses. "Someday, and that day may never come, I'll ask you to do a service for me."

The Ox-Bow Incident

"Hanging's any man's business that's around."

The Ox-Bow Incident is a 1940 western novel by Walter Van Tilburg Clark in which two drifters are drawn into a lynch mob to find and hang three men presumed to be rustlers and the killers of a local man. In 1943, the novel was adapted into a movie of the same name. The movie differs in some details from the novel but both are powerful.

The story takes place in 1885, and begins with two cowboys, Art Croft and Gil Carter, riding into the town of Bridger's Wells. They go into Canby's Saloon and find the atmosphere is tense, partly due to recent incidents of cattle rustling. News is brought that a local named Larry Kinkaid has been murdered and a large number of cattle have been stolen. The townspeople begin to form a posse. Local men, Osgood and Davies, send for Judge Tyler to try to defuse the situation but the rancher, Tetley, arrives and incites them to further action. As the posse sets out, the judge warns that the men must be brought back alive to stand trial.

The posse finds cattle bearing Kincaid's brand and three men sleeping on the ground around a campfire: an old, raving man named Alva Hardwick; a Mexican named Juan Martinez, who claims to be unable to understand English; and the young Donald Martin. Tetley interrogates them. Martin says that he purchased the cattle and that Kincaid was to send the bill of sale at a later date. He says Kincaid was alive when he left him.

Most are skeptical, and more so when they discover the Mexican has a pistol engraved with Kincaid's name—which he claims he purchased. No one believes him, and a vote is taken on whether the men should be hanged or taken back to face justice in the town. Five of the men are opposed to the hanging, arguing that a court of law should decide if they are guilty. They are out-voted, with the others fearing the delay and uncertainty of justice in a court of law. When sunrise approaches, the condemned men are placed upon their horses with nooses around their necks and hanged.

After the lynching, the riders head back toward town. Along the way, they meet Sheriff Risley, Judge Tyler, and, much to their surprise, the supposedly murdered Lawrence Kinkaid, who confirms that he'd sold the cattle to Martin. The infuriated sheriff declares he will have the entire mob up on charges for murder. However, after staring down each member of the lynch mob one at a time, he declares that he will pretend he saw nobody and knows nothing. He forms a posse and they go out in search of the real rustlers.

As in *The Godfather*, the perception of the law and the justice system for many of the characters is that it is weak, slow and ineffectual, and that it favors the rich at the expense of the average person. For many of them, the law is seen, not as their protector, but rather as their oppressor. The judge is portrayed as symbolic of that system. There is no question that the core of the justice the men in the posse seek is revenge, or retribution.

They are concerned with deterrence and don't think the law will give it. When the leader of the vigilante posse is told they should wait for Judge Tyler, be balks. He says that if they wait for Tyler, "there won't be one head of cattle left in the meadows by the time we get justice." "He also suggests that the slow and ineffective enforcement of law is an open invitation to "every thieving Mex and Indian and runaway Reb in the whole territory."

Another man points out that the law doesn't protect people like them, but rather those like the railroad men, those "plush-bottomed, soft-handed bastards, who couldn't even drive their own wagons." That's the kind of law, he says, they are being asked to wait for, "the kind that'll give a murderer plenty of time to get away and cover up, then help him find his excuses by the book."

One man, Davies, tries to reason with the man. He acknowledges that "[l]egal action's not always just." Then he asks the man what he thought real justice was, and eventually gets the answer that, "It's seeing that everybody gets what's coming to him."

Davies agrees that's a pretty good definition. "But according to whom?" he asks.

Again, the man eventually says, "We do. The rest of us. The straight ones."

Davies agrees again, "so long as the 'we' is large enough to include everybody." He asks further, "But how do we decide what the person has coming?"

The man responds, "You just know that things like rustling and murder is wrong." When pressed further by Davies as to how we know that for sure, the man says, "because they are against the law."

Which makes Davies' point about it taking a larger "we" than just those in the posse, or the valley, to justify a hanging, and that the only way to make it right was to let the law decide. If, he argues, they hang the men without doing what the law requires, then they are violating the law and should be hanged themselves.

When asked who would hang them, Davies replies, maybe nobody, and that makes their crime worse than the murderer's. "His act puts him outside the law but keeps the law intact. Ours would weaken the law." The greater "we" could absorb a few unpunished criminals, but not unpunished extra-legal justice.

He says, "Law is more than the words that put it on the books; law is more than any decisions that may be made from it; law is more than any particular code of it stated at any one time or in any one place or nation; more than any man, lawyer or judge, sheriff or jailer, who may represent it. True law, the code of justice, the essence of our sensations of right and wrong, is the conscience of society. It has taken thousands of years to develop, and it is the greatest, the most distinguishing quality which has evolved with mankind. None of man's temples, none of his tools, his arts, his sciences, nothing else he has grown to, is so great a thing as his justice, his sense of justice. The true law is something in itself; it is the spirit of the moral nature of man; it is an existence apart. If we can touch God at all, where do we touch him save our conscience? And what is the conscience of any man save his little fragment of the conscience of all men in all time?"

Couldn't have said it better myself.

It's a little strange, though, you have to admit, for this guy to be spouting out so philosophically to men getting a lynch mob together. Stretches believability for the story a bit, but I have to say, it's a pretty good argument as to what justice is and how noble a virtue it is. In addition to what the author hits you over the head with, there are other themes going on here. We see the pressure, or tyranny, of the majority, in this case, a mob mentality, to go along. As the leader says, "We must act as a unit, and then we need fear no reprisals."

And Gil and Art, who have just ridden into town, are caught up in it. Part of it is that they are strangers in town, and thus automatically under suspicion. Part of it is they want to be a moderating influence perhaps. As Gil responds later when told to butt out, that it really is none of his business, "Hanging's any man's business that's around." It doesn't get him anywhere as the men still hang. And while Gil and Art and Davies, and a couple of more are willing to vote against the hangings, they are not prepared to use force to prevent them.

The only price exacted on the men is on their consciences. In the last scene of the movie they are all standing around at the bar, looking glum. But when Art is told that they were raising $500 to send to Martin's wife, he remarks, "Not a bad price to pay for a husband that don't know any better than to buy cattle in the spring without a bill of sale."

Even though the others give him a look, you can feel the beginning of the rationalizing or minimizing that will eventually absolve them in their own minds. Perhaps, perhaps not.

It's a little off point, and certainly not on the scale of a lynch mob, but I am reminded of *Ox Bow* today, when a small group of students decides that a person who speaks hate is not allowed to speak on their campus, even though the law, i.e., the First Amendment, allows it. They don't make a legal challenge, maybe because, as in *Ox Bow*, they don't believe the law will give them justice. Instead, they take it upon themselves to get it. Shouldn't it take a larger "we" to decide who can speak and who can't?

If you have ever surfed *YouTube* for videos featuring judges, you will find plenty. And the most popular ones seem to be judges unloading on defendants, or being rude and disrespectful to people before them. One that made the rounds a few years ago involved a case in which charges of domestic battery had to be dismissed because the alleged victim failed to show for trial. The judge had the woman brought before her to show cause why she shouldn't be held in contempt of court for failing to obey a lawfully served subpoena.

The woman is crying and trying to explain that she was going through a rough time and had a lot of anxiety. She really wanted the State to drop the charges, she said, and just get on with her life. The judge was not moved, and held her in contempt and imposed a sentence of three days in jail. You should watch the video to get the flavor of what was happening. It's probably still on *You Tube*, as is the later public reprimand the judge received from The Florida Supreme Court. There is also a video from Nancy Grace's show where she expresses outrage and says the governor of Florida—yes, it was in Florida—should remove the judge. The incident was also used in a class at our judicial college about judicial ethics, and what judges should not do.

Now, I make no apologies for this judge and do not condone her conduct. She was intemperate and she berated and belittled the woman in front of her, and she should have been called on it. But what gets lost in the discussion, the outrage expressed at a judge "throwing the victim in jail," is this: How do we know that the woman was, in fact, a victim?

Under our law, a person accused of a crime is presumed innocent unless and until, the government can present evidence to a jury sufficient to convince them beyond a reasonable doubt that the defendant is guilty of what he has been accused of.

That's why we have trials. And this woman's action in refusing to obey the subpoena, meant there would be no trial, as her testimony was crucial. There is an important public interest to protect in making sure that people do not decide when and under what circumstances they will obey the law, even if they are an alleged victim of a crime. And indeed, that's what she was, legally, an alleged victim, because the allegations against the defendant had not been proven.

Now, the defendant probably was guilty. Experience and human nature suggest it, and that's what advocates, indeed, most of the public, assume in these situations. But, just as in *Ox Bow,* there is a danger to such assumptions, in deciding what should happen without giving an accused the protection of due process.

If a person supposedly witnessed a murder, or a robbery, or a car theft, or most other crimes, we expect that person to cooperate with law enforcement and prosecutors in giving testimony when required to see that justice is done in the case. We may understand reluctance, and we want those in contact with the witness to be respectful, and understanding of the reluctance, but we also understand that we can't just let witnesses, even those who were allegedly the victim of the crime, decide whether or not they will testify.

There is a common misconception, as reinforced on television and in films, that the victim can decline to prosecute. You've seen it many times, the frustrated cop who complains, "Yeah, she refused to press charges." In reality, the decision to prosecute or not is for the prosecutor to make, with due consideration for the wishes of the alleged victim. That's because as a society we have an interest in seeing that violators of the law are punished, that they and others are deterred from similar conduct in the future.

In reality, you could force a witness to obey a summons, hold them in contempt if they refuse to testify, but you can't make the witness testify consistent with their original complaint or statement. Domestic violence cases are a special breed. In almost no other case do you have the alleged victim begging the State to drop charges, or retracting their statements when they get to trial. It's what makes these types of cases frustrating for prosecutors sometimes. I heard one prosecutor explain that he treats it like a murder case, that is, you prepare it with the assumption you won't have a victim to testify at trial.

What the judge should have done, in my opinion, is to bring the woman in and let her explain why she didn't obey the subpoena, go over all the options available to her, i.e., what she could have done to address any issues she had. The judge could have made the point she wanted in a manner that showed compassion and understanding of the woman's situation, while still emphasizing the importance of witnesses obeying subpoenas. If the judge found her explanation insufficient and thought contempt of court was appropriate, she could have required her to do some community service hours, preferably for an organization advocating against domestic violence.

Lonesome Dove

"I didn't see no line, Gus."

In *The Ox Bow Incident*, we feel uncomfortable at what is happening. We know intuitively that it is wrong, that the men should be taken in for a trial, despite the expressed concern of some of the men that the courts are weak and ineffectual, that justice will not be done unless they do it themselves. The uncomfortable feeling about what is happening is confirmed when we learn that they were completely innocent.

What if, instead, we knew they were guilty? That's what we have in a scene from *Lonesome Dove*, a novel by Larry McMurtry which was made into a mini-series for television, starring Tommy Lee Jones (Woodrow) and Robert Duval (Gus) as former Texas Rangers taking a herd of cattle to market. A lot happens along the way, including a graphic depiction of a lynching of four men.

We know the men are guilty of horse stealing and the murder of five men, because we see it happen. Three of the men are brothers, the oldest of which is the leader and particularly cruel. He is not content to just murder the farmers but he burns their bodies as well. He and his brothers are not, to put it mildly, sympathetic characters.

The fourth man is a friend and former colleague of Gus and Woodrow, Jake, who had been with the cattle drive for a while, but struck out on his own. Jake is a hard drinker and a bit of a ladies' man and he likes to gamble, but he is not in the same class as the others. As he explains, he decided to ride with them just to get through the Indian Territory without getting scalped. He was going to leave them as soon as he could. In fact, we have seen that he was under some duress or coercion from the others to go along, or maybe be their next victim.

Woodrow, Gus and the others are faced with a difficult task. Jake is their friend, but their code dictates that he is guilty, just like the others and, just like them, must hang for his crimes. As Gus puts it when Jake says he was planning on leaving the other men, "I wish you'd left a little sooner." He tells Jake that he crossed the line.

Jake says, "I didn't see no line, Gus, I was just trying to get through the territory." "I'm sure that's right," Gus says. Nevertheless, they all know he has to hang. It pains them all but they do it. In typical manly fashion, no one says anything about it, but they appreciate that he dies with dignity—he tells them he'd much rather be hung by his friends than strangers, then spurs his own horse so Gus won't have to do it. Woodrow says, "Let's dig him a grave." It's their sign of respect for him even though he fell in with outlaws.

It's a poignant scene. This is certainly rough, harsh, frontier justice. There is no time, no need, to take them to the "proper authorities." The code has its integrity, as well, as it makes no exceptions for friends. You commit the crime, you receive the punishment. But, although we know the brothers are scum of the earth, that they are guilty of heinous murder and deserve to die, there is in some of us at least a twinge of discomfort at the summary execution of these men. After all, the lessen we learn from *Ox Bow* is we can could make a terrible mistake by acting too quickly in determining who is guilty and meting out punishment.

Gus and the others also seem to ignore a principle of justice that many recognize, a variation of the theme of proportionality we saw in *The Godfather*. Closely related is the notion that we should apportion the blame among members of a group who commit a crime, depending on their individual behaviors. For example, the person who drives the getaway car in a bank robbery is legally just as guilty of Felony Murder as the person who carries the gun inside and shoots the bank guard who tries to stop the robbery. But is he as morally culpable? Many would say no, that the person who actually pulled the trigger is more culpable and should receive the harsher punishment.

Here, Jake didn't want to participate in the murders. He thought about intervening in fact, but he faced retaliation from the others in the group. You could make an argument that he was coerced to commit the crimes, or under duress, recognized legal defenses to such crimes. At the very least it is a mitigating factor when considering an appropriate punishment.

Unfortunately for Jake, but in the interest of making a better story, he is lumped in with the others. I mean, it would have been much less satisfying for the story if they spared Jake, found some other punishment for him. No, that wouldn't work at all from a story standpoint. And, indeed, many people may feel that there was no reason to differentiate between Jake and the others and that his hanging along with them was just. Woodrow and the others certainly felt so. At the very least, the result is not nearly the tragic one we encounter in *Ox Bow*. In both instances, the executioners act outside the formal law. In one, they hang innocent men. In the other, even if we accept that at least the brothers deserved hanging, it still makes you a bit uncomfortable because of the summary nature of it and the failure to consider any possible defenses or mitigating facts for one of them.

Billy Budd

"We deal not with justice, but with the law."

We're not done with hangings yet.

In contrast to *Ox Bow* and *Lonesome Dove*, the hanging in *Billy Budd* is done with maritime due process and strict adherence to the law of the seas, and administered through the "proper authorities." There is no doubt as to the legality of what is done, only as to its justness.

Billy Budd, Sailor, is a novella by Herman Melville, first published posthumously in London in 1924. Acclaimed by British critics as a masterpiece when published, it quickly took its place as a classic literary work in the United States.

It was adapted into a film in 1962, produced, directed, co-written, and starring Peter Ustinov, with Terence Stamp receiving an Academy Award nomination in his film debut. It also starred David McCullum, an actor known to fans of the television show, The Man from Uncle, as Illya Kuryakin, and as Dr. Donald Mallard ("Ducky") in the series, NCIS.

Billy Budd is a seaman impressed into service aboard the HMS Bellipotent in the year 1797, when the Royal Navy was reeling from two major mutinies and was threatened by the Revolutionary French Republic's military ambitions. Billy is an innocent, with good looks and a natural charisma that make him popular with the crew. His only physical defect is a stutter which grows worse when under intense emotion.

Billy gets sideways with the ship's master-at-arms, Claggart, who, for no apparent reason other than he envies Billy's good looks and his popularity, falsely charges Billy with conspiracy to mutiny. When he makes his case to Captain Vere, Billy is unable to respond due to his stutter. In his frustration he strikes out at Claggart, who falls, hits his head and dies as a result.

Vere convenes a court-martial to decide the matter. The court-martial panel is inclined to find Billy not guilty. They do not believe Claggart's charge of conspiracy and think Billy justified in his response, his stuttering causing him to respond physically rather than verbally to the charges.

But when the panel readies to vote not guilty, Captain Vere intervenes, reminding them of their duty as officers under the law. "Your verdict sets him free, and so would I wish to do. But are we free to choose as we would if we were private citizens? The Admiralty has its code. Do you think it cares who Budd is? Who you and I are?"

He points out that Budd struck a superior officer, and under the Mutiny Act's provisions, at sea, in time of war, the mere fact of the blow would be enough to hang him, be it fatal or not. To the call for mercy or pity, he answers that they "cannot have warm hearts betraying heads which should be cool."

One of the officers argues that when Claggart told the captain his lies, "the case immediately went beyond military justice."

"There, Seymour," the captain responds, "you reveal the whole weakness of your argument. Here, nothing is beyond the scope of military justice….The gold we wear shows that we serve the king... ...the law. For the term of my active life, I am bound by an oath I took... ...when I was half the age of any of you here…. Yes, but... ...gentlemen, you took that oath as well. There's no escape."

"Couldn't we... ...mitigate the penalty if we find him guilty?"

"No, Ratcliffe, the penalty is prescribed. Our consciences are private matters, Ratcliffe, but we are public men. Dare we give our consciences precedence over the code that made us officers? And which called this case to trial? Dare we? No, sir. Wyatt... ...we do not deal with justice here, but with the law."

"Was not the one conceived to serve the other?"

"You think Seymour, Ratcliffe and I wouldn't save the boy... ...if we could find a way consistent with our duty? Well, perhaps you can do this. Can you do this? Speak, man. Speak. Show us how. Save him, Wyatt, and you save us all."

The officer is unable to come up with a good counter argument, and the panel votes to hang Billy. For his part, Billy is remarkably philosophical about the whole thing. When the captain pleads for him to be angry, to hate him for what he has done, tells him that hatred will ease his fear, Billy says, "I'm not afraid, sir. I did my duty. You're doing yours."

The captain's final observation is that, "...if the sacrifice of Billy Budd... ... has served to make men more conscious of justice... ... then he will not have died in vain. Men are perishable things... ... but justice will live as long as the human soul... ... and the law, as long as the human mind."

Thus, in sharp contrast to *Ox Bow*, which extolls result over process, Billy Budd extolls process over result. In both cases, a person we see as "innocent" is hanged. In the former, we clearly can conclude that justice was not done, but rather corrupted, hijacked by vigilantes. There will be disagreement as to whether justice is done for Budd. But as Captain Vere observes, "We deal in law here, not justice."

For those whose duty it is to enforce the law, even where the result is unjust and repulsive to them, the tension between law and justice and law and morality is palpable. Arguably, by strictly adhering to the law in an individual case, justice as a whole is made stronger for the group. That does not, however, make it any easier for those who must enforce the law. And, depending on where you land on the ends vs. means continuum, you might agree with the reply of Mr. Bumble, the unhappy spouse of a domineering wife in Charles Dickens' *Oliver Twist,* when he is told in court that "...the law supposes that your wife acts under your direction." "If the law supposes that," says Mr. Bumble, squeezing his hat emphatically in both hands, "then the law is a ass – a idiot".

Letters from a Birmingham Jail

"An unjust law is no law at all."

This was an essay Martin Luther King wrote in response to an open letter penned by eight clergymen in Alabama and published in a Birmingham newspaper, criticizing his campaign of coordinated marches and sit-ins against racism and racial segregation in the city. He wrote the "letter" while jailed in Birmingham for violating an injunction issued by a local judge.

He began by responding to the criticism that he and his fellow activists were "outsiders" causing trouble in the streets of Birmingham. To this, King referred to his responsibility as the leader of the Southern Christian Leadership Conference, which had numerous affiliated organizations throughout the South. "I was invited" by our Birmingham affiliate "because injustice is here."

Referring to his belief that all communities and states were interrelated, King wrote, "Injustice anywhere is a threat to justice everywhere. We are caught in an inescapable network of mutuality, tied in a single garment of destiny. Whatever affects one directly, affects all indirectly ... Anyone who lives inside the United States can never be considered an outsider anywhere within its bounds."

The clergymen also disapproved of tensions created by public actions such as sit-ins and marches. To this, King confirmed that he and his fellow demonstrators were indeed using nonviolent direct action in order to create "constructive" tension. This tension was intended to compel meaningful negotiation with the white power structure, without which true civil rights could never be achieved. Citing previous failed negotiations, King wrote that the Black community was left with no alternative, observing, "We know through painful experience that freedom is never voluntarily given by the oppressor; it must be demanded by the oppressed."

The clergymen also disapproved of the timing of public actions. In response, King said that in the broader scope of history, "'Wait' has almost always meant 'Never.'" Declaring that African Americans had waited for these God-given and constitutional rights long enough, King quoted Chief Justice Earl Warren, who said in 1958 that "justice too long delayed is justice denied."

Against the clergymen's assertion that demonstrations could be illegal, King argued that not only was civil disobedience justified in the face of unjust laws, but it was necessary and even patriotic. The answer, he writes, lies in the fact that there are two types of laws: just and unjust.

"I would be the first to advocate obeying just laws. One has not only a legal but a moral responsibility to obey just laws. Conversely, one has a moral responsibility to disobey unjust laws. I would agree with St. Augustine that an unjust law is no law at all. Any law not rooted in "eternal law and natural law" is not just, while any law that "uplifts human personality" is.

He argued that segregation laws were immoral and unjust "because segregation distorts the soul and damages the personality. It gives the segregator a false sense of superiority and the segregated a false sense of inferiority." Even some just laws, he wrote, such as permit requirements for public marches, were unjust when used to uphold an unjust system.

"I submit that an individual who breaks a law that conscience tells him is unjust, and who willingly accepts the penalty of imprisonment in order to arouse the conscience of the community over its injustice, is in reality expressing the highest respect for law."

The letter/essay was, and is, a powerful, eloquent piece of literature. The man was truly gifted as a writer and orator. And there is much in there for thought about justice for our purposes. I don't know that I can agree with the premise that an unjust law is not a law at all. It may be just semantics, but if we define a law as a rule enacted by a legitimate authority, then a law is a law, whether just or unjust. His litmus test, though, of how to determine if a law is just or unjust, seems a pretty good rule of thumb.

And he nicely pulls in the idea that there is a natural, organic or divine law by which any man-made law must be measured, a la John Locke, and if the latter conflicts with the former, it is not a just law. A similar conviction is expressed by the defense lawyer in *Inherit the Wind*, whose client is charged with teaching evolution to his students. "You cannot fairly administer a wicked law."

Also compelling is his argument that we have a moral duty to disobey an unjust law. In fact, he says, when done openly, with a willingness to accept the penalty, so as to prick the conscience of fellow citizens, it shows profound respect for law and justice. This seems much more ethical and moral than those who justify breaking the law when it doesn't achieve justice in their view, but they do it in secret, not openly, and try their best to avoid the punishment.

Judges and others tasked with enforcing the law have different responsibilities. Where there is wiggle room, they can try to eliminate or minimize the conflict between the written law and the natural law, or between law and justice. But if there is no wiggle room, if the law is clear, they must either do their sworn, legal duty, or openly disobey it and accept the consequences. That is the moral thing to do. Hence the officers' dilemma in Billy Budd. You shouldn't scheme to find some way around what the law requires. You should resign before you do that, for as Davies argued in *Ox Bow*, if you act under color of law while you break it, you make the law weaker.

And a judge should not recuse (remove herself from a case) every time she is faced with a conflict between what she thinks is just and what the law requires. That just puts the burden on some other judge. The judge can express in her order her disagreement with the law, lamenting the injustice that results, and urge the legislative body to reconsider it. But she should not contort her brain and her words to rationalize, ignoring what is a clear duty to uphold and enforce the law, as she swore to do.

Earthly Justice

"I often reflected about justice, but I never allowed myself to discuss it with my father…."

After successful careers in retail and advertising, Elliott Stanley Goldman turned to writing. Although he wrote one novel, he is best known for his short stories, having published more stories in *The Atlantic Monthly* in a thirty-year period than any other writer. His story collection, *Earthly Justice*, won the William Goyen Prize for literature. Late in life, he retired to South Orleans on Cape Cod where he continued to write short stories well into his eighties. He died in 2013, weeks short of his 100th birthday.

In *Earthly Justice*, the narrator tells of an event from his childhood, when his aunt was killed and his uncle charged with her murder. His father urges caution in jumping to conclusions, and patience in letting the justice system get to the truth. The boy senses the hollowness of the father's preaching, and he notes, "I began to understand how words say things that aren't in them. Words reach for meanings that are already inside the hearer." But he also accepts it on a face level. "We had a stake in the values of organized society."

They follow the development of the case and the trial. There is some pretty good evidence against the uncle but the jury returns a verdict of not guilty. The father seems to accept the verdict, says they just have to look harder for the real killer or killers. "I wasn't hired to be God," he says. He expresses sympathy for the uncle, who had been through an ordeal, and he hoped he could get on with his life.

But he has hidden his true feelings. He invites the uncle to come fishing, where he intentionally leads him to a dangerous part of the lake. The uncle loses his balance, falls in and drowns, while the father looks the other way. All of this, unbeknownst to the father, is witnessed by the son, who has come to join them.

For obvious reasons, the event has a lasting effect on the boy. He never lets on to anyone, especially his father, what he has witnessed. He wrestles with guilt for his inaction, at the lake, and afterwards. He notes, "I often reflected about justice, but I never allowed myself to discuss it with my father, fearing that one word would take me to another until I reached the one that I would regret." Nine years later, the real killer turns himself in and confesses.

It is a poignant story eloquently told, and has parallels to the other stories we've looked at with the tension or conflict between the public law and the private code of morality. Like the undertaker in *The Godfather*, the father, dissatisfied with the result in the court, resorts to self-help. But just as in *The Ox Bow Incident*, rather than avenging his sister's murder, he murders an innocent person.

And that makes a difference in how we judge him and his actions, doesn't it? We are sympathetic to the frustration, and had we been sure the uncle was guilty, we would not judge him too harshly. He did what a lot of people would want to do, who want the guilty person punished, but do not act. It might be because of respect for the rules, the process, even if we don't agree with this particular result. It might be fear of getting caught, and punished ourselves. But when we learn the uncle was innocent—of murder anyway, if not infidelity—our sympathy takes a nose dive.

The way he exacts his revenge is a little passive aggressive, too. He doesn't confront the uncle and shoot him. He sets the stage and lets mother nature do the real dirty work. It gives him plausible deniability if a suspicious detective starts asking questions. Not exactly the open disobedience of the law and loving acceptance of the punishment espoused by Martin Luther King in *Letter from a Birmingham Jail*. Of course, this is a little different as there is no question of the justness of the law, only a disagreement as to the result of its application. After a while, the father seems to return to a normal life, though we don't know if his conscience bothers him.

The boy, the narrator, feels guilty but it's hard to judge him guilty of anything but loyalty to his father. His father did wrong. He knows that. But at least the father acted out of a sense of justice, of enforcing a private code of justice and morality. And no matter how wrong his father was, the maxim that blood is thicker than water is a strong cultural value not to be discarded lightly. As in *Ox Bow*, there is no legal sanction for killing the uncle. The only punishment for both father and son is psychological, one of conscience.

A Few Good Men

"You can't handle the truth!"

This dramatic courtroom thriller, which was released in 1992, pits Tom Cruise, as Lt. Daniel Kaffee, against Jack Nicholson, as Colonel Nathan Jessup, in one of the most entertaining cross examinations in film history. Kaffee represents two Marines who have been accused of murdering a colleague, PFC Santiago. The defense theory is that Jessup ordered a "code red" as to Santiago, meaning he was to be hazed and forced to leave, and that because of an unforeseen medical condition, Santiago died as a result of the hazing. The problem is, nobody at the base at Guantanamo will acknowledge the code red.

At trial, Jessup takes the stand. Kaffee points out some internal inconsistencies in his testimony; Jessup testifies that Santiago was being shipped out at six 'o'clock the next morning, but he hadn't packed a bag nor called anyone to let them know; Jessup says he was being shipped out because he was in danger, but he had previously testified that he gave an order that Santiago was not to be touched and emphasized that his orders are always followed, so that Santiago shouldn't have been in any danger. In the final, dramatic confrontation, Kaffee says he thinks he is entitled to some answers.

JESSEP *You want answers?!*

KAFFEE *I want the truth.*

JESSEP *You can't handle the truth!*

And nobody moves.

JESSEP (continuing) *Son, we live in a world that has walls. And those walls have to be guarded by men with guns. Who's gonna do it? You? You, Lt. Weinberg? I have a greater responsibility than you can possibly fathom. You weep for Santiago and you curse the marines. You have that luxury. You have the luxury of not knowing what I know: That Santiago's death, while tragic, probably saved lives. And my existence, while grotesque and incomprehensible to you, saves lives.*

You don't want the truth. Because deep down, in places you don't talk about at parties, you want me on that wall. You need me there. (boasting) We use words like honor, code, loyalty... we use these words as the backbone to a life spent defending something. You use 'em as a punchline.

I have neither the time nor the inclination to explain myself to a man who rises and sleeps under the blanket of the very freedom I provide, then questions the manner in which I provide it. I'd prefer you just said thank you and went on your way. Otherwise, I suggest you pick up a weapon and stand a post. Either way, I don't give a damn what you think you're entitled to.

This, I think, is a firmly-held belief by many persons who we expect to protect us, military persons being the most extreme example. Law enforcement officers fit into this category as well. And many of us can relate to what the colonel says. We want these people (law enforcement officers) to do what is necessary to protect us. And in most cases, we don't want to know exactly how they do it. We'd rather not know when they bend the rules or even break them. We understand it's a tough job, one we don't want, and we don't want to second guess them.

But that's because we don't think we'll ever be the victim of such misconduct. If you've ever been on the receiving end of police harassment or intimidation, or physical brutality, or had them plant evidence or lie to make a case against you, you have a different opinion. Most people would like to think that our law enforcement officers are all strong, ethical people, but we know that's not always the case.

In recent years, with the proliferation of cell phones and social media, it has become more difficult to hide from this reality. Those places "we don't talk about at parties" are more exposed. Yes, we want them on the wall. We need them on the wall. But we are embarrassed when we have to face the evidence of misconduct and crimes committed by those persons. Even then, we want to give them the benefit of the doubt, because otherwise we have to admit to our own complicity. In fact, the law gives law enforcement officers the benefit of the doubt through legal means by affording qualified immunity for all but the most egregious acts that violate the law, the Constitution, or a person's civil rights.

This harkens back to what was observed by Davies in *The Ox Bow Incident* about justice being more endangered by those who do wrong under the color of law, than by those who act outside the law. I do think that those whose job it is to enforce the law, including law enforcement officers and judges, have a special position of trust. When they are found to have violated the law, it is a serious violation of that trust, and it lessens the moral authority of all officers and judges. It is similar to what has been said about a reputation: It takes years to obtain a good reputation and seconds to lose it.

Riggs v Palmer

"No one shall be permitted to...acquire property by his own crime."

Let's take a look at how your philosophy of justice is shaping up with consideration of some real cases. For those of you who insist that judges should not "legislate from the bench" and speak with disdain about activist judges, let's see where you land after considering the facts in the case of *Riggs v Palmer*, 115 NY 506 Court of Appeals of New York, 1889.

Francis B. Palmer made his last will and testament in which he gave small legacies to his two daughters and the remainder of his estate to his grandson, Elmer Palmer. At the date of the will and until the death of Francis, Elmer lived with him as a member of his family, and at his death was sixteen years old. Elmer knew of the provisions made in his favor in the will and, seeking to prevent his grandfather from revoking such provisions, Elmer murdered him by poisoning him. The other beneficiaries sued, arguing that Elmer should not be able to take under the will, having murdered the testator.

Elmer argued that the law was clear. A will, duly executed and admitted to probate could only be changed or modified under certain listed conditions, and the murder of the testator by a beneficiary was not one of them. The plaintiffs acknowledged that, if literally construed, the statute would allow the grandson to inherit, but that such an absurd result could not have been intended by the legislature, and that the court should not so interpret it. They relied upon the maxim of equity that a person should not be allowed to benefit from his wrongful conduct. The trial court agreed with Elmer and dismissed the case.

On appeal, the members of the court split as to the proper ruling. The majority took the view of the plaintiffs and reversed the trial court. In their view, a statute should not be interpreted so as to lead to an absurd result, one that no rational legislature could have intended. Had the legislature considered the particular circumstances of this case, they would have made provision in the statute to address it.

"What could be more unreasonable than to suppose that it was the legislative intention...that they should have operation in favor of one who murdered his ancestor that he might speedily come into the possession of his estate? Such an intention is inconceivable. We need not, therefore, be much troubled by the general language contained in the laws.

"Besides, all laws as well as all contracts may be controlled in their operation and effect by general, fundamental maxims of the common law. No one shall be permitted to profit by his own fraud, or to take advantage of his own wrong, or to found any claim upon his own iniquity, or to acquire property by his own crime. These maxims are dictated by public policy, have their foundation in universal law administered in all civilized countries, and have nowhere been superseded by statutes."

The dissent took a different view, similar to that espoused by Captain Vere in *Billy Budd*. The maxim that one should not be permitted to take advantage of his own wrong is one of equity, not law, the judge said, "and, if I believed that the decision of the question could be affected by considerations of an equitable nature, I should not hesitate to assent to views which commend themselves to the conscience. But the matter does not lie within the domain of conscience. We are bound by the rigid rules of law, which have been established by the legislature, and within the limits of which the determination of this question is confined."

And, just as Captain Vere urged, the dissent argued that the court had a duty to adhere to the law, not to conscience or ideas of equity or justice. The question, he said, is whether a testamentary disposition could be altered after the testator's death in a manner not provided for in the law as written. The answer to him was clear, that the law left "no room for the exercise of an equitable jurisdiction by courts over such matters."

The judge pointed out that other jurisdictions had provisions in their law that disallowed inheritance by one who murdered the testator, and the Legislature certainly could have done so here, if that was the intent. "In the absence of such legislation here, the courts are not empowered to institute such a system of remedial justice. If, in light of this case, the legislature decided to amend the statute, that is their prerogative, not the court's."

So, which side do you come down on? Reasonable people can disagree, obviously, but your answer will tell you if you are, in fact, a "strict constructionist" as some of you probably insist you are, with your disdain for "activist judges" who "legislate from the bench." Perhaps you think it is all right to "legislate from the bench" if the legislature didn't get it right. Or do you apply the law as it is and let the legislature remedy its own mistake, if mistake it was. Go look at your ends v means scale again and see if you are still comfortable with where you placed yourself.

My take is that the majority's view takes the court outside its lane. It is clearly re-writing the statute. Now, most people would agree that the application of the law in this case led to an absurd result. People who kill their relatives so as to speed up their inheritance, shouldn't get it. But the maxim is too loose, and itself is subject to interpretation. In another situation, a court's determination that a particular result from the application of a statute is "absurd" might not be met with universal agreement. And in that case, respect for the court as an impartial arbitrator suffers. As a practical matter, the legislature can address the matter whichever way the court rules, if they disagree.

There is another maxim, or more precisely, a principle of statutory interpretation, that tells judges that it is not their place to pass upon the wisdom of legislation. And to me, that's the safer, more stable approach in the long run. The judge can lament the injustice of the law's application in a case, and suggest that the Legislature remedy it, if they agree, but should not presume to know what the Legislature did or did not intend.

Let's alter the facts a bit and see if it makes a difference to you. Suppose that after the grandfather's death, we find a note in with his will and other important papers. The note is clearly in his handwriting and it states: "I know that my grandson has been poisoning me. I am okay with that as I don't have much time left anyway. I still love him very much and want to provide for him when I am gone. Should anyone else discover his actions in causing my death, let it be known that I still wish for him to inherit as prescribed in my Last Will and Testament."

In the face of the clear language in the statute, and the clear intent of the testator, do you still want to side with the majority?

Stand Your Ground

Welcome to the Wild West

As a further example, let's look at a case I presided over involving a newly enacted revision of the self-defense statute, commonly called "Stand Your Ground." Here's the essence:

Two rival gangs passed each other in cars on the street. Both cars stopped and the occupants began firing at the others. There were bullet holes in the vehicles but no one was hurt. Both cars drove off.

One of the cars ended up at an apartment complex. The occupants fully expected the others to come looking for them, so they stood by their vehicle with their firearms (including an AK-47 legally purchased by an 18-year-old) and waited. And sure enough, the occupants of the other vehicle rounded up some other gang members and a caravan began driving slowly into the apartment complex. They exchanged gunfire again.

In the resulting shootout, a 15-year-old in one of the incoming cars is shot dead. Several people are charged with murder and they all file motions to dismiss claiming self-defense. All claimed that they were legally in a place they had a right to be. And they were. So, it boiled down to who fired first. From independent witnesses residing in the complex, based on the types of weapons used and the sound heard, I determined this crucial fact and made my ruling.

So, even though there was ample opportunity to avoid it, what we had was two gangs voluntarily engaging in a shootout on a residential street and at an apartment complex. And the prevailing case law suggested that if one of the participants was acting in self-defense, fired and missed, and the bullet hit and killed a toddler in the apartment complex, he would not be liable. And he certainly was not liable for killing one of the other participants.

My order started off by observing that the case perhaps represented a situation that the authors of the law had not contemplated, i.e., giving cover for gangs shooting it out on the streets like the wild west. I could have said such an interpretation would lead to an absurd result, and that it didn't apply in this situation, but I didn't see that as my place. Maybe such situations were contemplated by the law's drafters and they were okay with it.

So, I outlined all the problems I saw in the application of the law. Procedurally, the prior version of the self-defense law made it an affirmative defense which the defendant could raise at trial with the jury deciding the issue. An affirmative defense is one that says, even if what you say I did is true, e.g., shot a person, I'm still not guilty because I acted in self-defense, and the law says that is a defense to the charge.

Under the statute as amended, a defendant could also raise this defense in a motion to dismiss which a judge would rule on based on a preponderance of the evidence standard. If the judge denied the motion, the defendant could still raise it with the jury. That meant that a defendant got two bites at the apple, with the same witnesses having to testify twice, and the lawyers and judge spending the additional time on the case.

In addition, if there are multiple defendants, as in my case, motions to dismiss may be filed at different times and may require multiple hearings. Depending on the evidence presented at each of those hearings, and the skill of the lawyer, some defendants may get a dismissal and others not, based on the same basic facts.

And that is what happened in my case. I granted some motions and denied others, based upon the evidence presented.

Most concerning to me, though, was the substantive change in the law. Before, you had an obligation to retreat (unless you were in your own house) if you could do so safely, before resorting to self-defense. Now, there was no duty to retreat if you were in a place you had a legal right to be, and you could use force in self-defense. Hence the monicker "Stand Your Ground."

What this meant, I said, was that you could purposely and intentionally insult a person, taunt them, goad them into attacking you, then kill them in self-defense so long as you were in a place you had a right to be and were otherwise engaged in lawful activity. It conjured up images of the wild west and a gunfight on the street. Which was not far off from what happened in my case.

I didn't like it, but I didn't see that I had a choice. My ruling, dismissing the case against some of the defendants, was the result mandated by an application of the law to the facts as I found them from the evidence. I pointed out in my order all of these problems with the law, or what I perceived as problems, and suggested that the Legislature might want to take another look. Perhaps these were unintended consequences of the law.

Apparently, they were not. Or perhaps no notice was taken of my observations. I don't know, but the only change subsequently made to the law was to make it even more difficult for the prosecution to get a case to a jury where a defendant moves to dismiss on grounds of self-defense. Before, the defendant had the burden to prove by a preponderance of the evidence that he had acted in self-defense in order to obtain a dismissal of the charge. Now, a prosecutor must convince a judge beyond a reasonable doubt that the defendant did not act in self-defense.

So, had I ruled that the Legislature could not possibly have intended the absurd result posed by this case, I would have been wrong. They had an opportunity to change it but didn't.

PGA v Martin

Is walking an essential part of the game of golf?

Are the competitors in a professional golf tournament customers for whom the PGA must make accommodation under the ADA (Americans with Disabilities Act) if they have a disability that makes it difficult to walk the course? This was the questions at the heart of another real case, *PGA Tour v. Martin*. 532 U.S. 661 (2001). Here is a summary:

The Petitioner, Professional Golf Association (PGA) sponsors professional golf tournaments conducted on three annual tours. The rules governing competition in tour events include the "Rules of Golf," which apply specifically to the PGA's professional tours and require players to walk the golf course during tournaments, except in "open" qualifying events for each tournament and on petitioner's senior tour. Respondent Martin is a talented golfer afflicted with a degenerative circulatory disorder that prevents him from walking golf courses. His disorder constitutes a disability under the Americans with Disabilities Act of 1990 (ADA), 42 U. S. C. §12101 et seq.

When Martin made a request, supported by detailed medical records, for permission to use a golf cart. Petitioner refused, and Martin filed this action under Title III of the ADA, which, among other things, requires an entity operating "public accommodations" to make "reasonable modifications" in its policies "when ... necessary to afford such ... accommodations to individuals with disabilities, *unless the entity can demonstrate that making such modifications would fundamentally alter the nature of such ... accommodations," §12182(b)(2)(A)(ii) (emphasis added).*

The PGA presented testimony from some of the greats of golf, including Arnold Palmer and Jack Nicholas, that the physical exertion of having to walk the course was an important part of the game. The trial judge disagreed, entering a permanent injunction requiring petitioner to permit Martin to use a cart. Among its rulings, that court found that the walking rule's purpose was to inject fatigue into the skill of shot-making, but that the fatigue injected by walking a golf course cannot be deemed significant under normal circumstances; determined that even with the use of a cart, the fatigue Martin suffers from coping with his disability is greater than the fatigue his able-bodied competitors endure from walking the course; and concluded that it would not fundamentally alter the nature of petitioner's game to accommodate Martin.

When it made its way to the Supreme Court, the majority agreed, concluding that golf courses, including play areas, are places of public accommodation during professional tournaments, and that permitting Martin to use a cart would not "fundamentally alter" the nature of those tournaments.

The dissent argued that a professional golf tournament is not a "public accommodation" and Martin was not a "customer" within the meaning of the ADA. "The common sense of the statute is that the content of the goods or services offered by a place of public accommodation is not regulated. A camera store may not refuse to sell cameras to a disabled person, but it is not required to stock cameras specially designed for such persons.

"If a shoe store wishes to sell shoes only in pairs it may; and if a golf tour (or a golf course) wishes to provide only walk-around golf, it may. The PGA TOUR cannot deny respondent *access* to that game because of his disability, but it need not provide him a game different (whether in its essentials or in its details) from that offered to everyone else.

"Agility, strength, speed, balance, quickness of mind, steadiness of nerves, intensity of concentration--these talents are not evenly distributed. No wild-eyed dreamer has ever suggested that the managing bodies of the competitive sports that test precisely these qualities should try to take account of the uneven distribution of God-given gifts when writing and enforcing the rules of competition. And I have no doubt Congress did not authorize misty-eyed judicial supervision of such a revolution."

What do you think? If you were on the Supreme Court, how would you rule, and why? Obviously, reasonable people can disagree. Even those on the highest court of the land see it differently. These are very smart people with much experience, the assistance of numerous law clerks, and the benefit of conferring with the other justices, after considering first the written and oral arguments of the attorneys representing the parties. If the law is the law, why was there disagreement as to its interpretation here?

Which side is right on this issue? Presumably, both the majority and the dissent believed, in good faith, that the law required very different results. Presumably, they saw no conflict between what the law required and justice. They just came to different conclusions about how the law was to be applied to the facts of the case. It seems that it all boils down to whether you think allowing someone to use a cart instead of walking during a golf tournament would fundamentally alter the nature of the game.

A justice of the Florida Supreme Court told me one time after he and his colleagues reversed me in a case, "Terry, we're not last because we're right. We're right because we're last." Well, the majority of the U.S. Supreme Court has the last word, so maybe they're right. But as I said before, what is fair and just is no one court or one person's prerogative.

For what it's worth, I align myself with the dissent. In virtually any sporting game, such as basketball, football, baseball, tennis, soccer, there is an object to the game, and a way to score or measure your relative success, to determine winners and losers. In basketball, you score points by getting the ball through a round hoop. In tennis, you score points by hitting a fuzzy ball with a racquet over a net and inside some lines more times than your opponent. You get the idea. In golf, the essential object of the game is to get a small ball into a small hole. If you've never seen Robin Williams' explanation of the origins of golf, check it out on YouTube. It's hilarious, if a bit profane.

In all of these sporting games, your skill at certain functions is important to your success. If you can consistently hit a ball coming at you at ninety miles per hour with a rounded stick, you should do well in baseball, assuming you are of at least average physical ability in other respects. And that's the point. Your skill at performing an essential function of the sport is only one part of the formula for success.

Your individual physical abilities, your speed, strength and endurance, are also very important. Even a very skilled and physically fit tennis player may get fatigued in the fifth set of a match, and begin to miss shots he would normally make. If his opponent is more fit, he has the edge. This is true for all such sports, including golf.

If you are playing for fun it doesn't matter that much. But if you are playing the sport at the highest level, for money, then it matters. If this were a public or private golf course open to the public, and Martin wanted to play a round of golf, I would perhaps agree that he should be allowed a cart, even if there was a rule against it. In that scenario, he is indeed a customer and should be given reasonable accommodation under the ADA. But if he wants to be a professional golfer and play for prize money, then he can't insist that the P.G.A. make an exception in its rules of competition just for him.

Well, as I say, reasonable people can differ, and the majority of the Supreme Court came down on the issue differently. There is no wrong answer in this respect. As Bob Dylan put it in *Tangled up in Blue*, "We always did feel the same. We just saw it from a different point of view."

I suggest that our idea of what the law is or means and what justice is or means is never set. It evolves over time. As suggested in *The Ox Bow Incident*, law and justice are found in the conscience of all men, a collective effort over time, informed by experience and reason. Inevitably, that effort brings changing notions of what is fair.

Rape and Fatherhood

The best interests of the child.

Consider this hypothetical, based on an actual case I had:

Paul Williams has filed a paternity action, seeking to establish himself as father of a two-year old child he only recently became aware of, and to establish an equal shared parenting arrangement. The mother, Alice Hoffman, acknowledges that Paul is the father, that they dated briefly, but says that he raped her and the child is the result of the ensuing pregnancy. She did not pursue criminal charges, but argues that by virtue of his criminal act he has forfeited any parenting rights he might have. She objects to any contact by him with the child. There is no corroborating evidence as to the rape, and Paul vehemently denies that he raped Alice. He has plenty of witnesses and evidence of his upstanding reputation in the community. He has a stable job and extended family in the area. There is no reason to think he can't otherwise parent a child.

Do you think Paul should be granted shared parenting with Alice? Why or why not? A lot is probably riding on whether you believe Alice or not. If you don't believe her, the decision is fairly easy. Paul should have shared parenting. Indeed, if you find that Alice acted out of spite for having been rejected by Paul, she was horrible for trying to deny the child the benefit of knowing his father. You might even give Paul primary parental responsibility. One of the factors a judge is supposed to consider in determining parenting arrangements is which parent is most likely to encourage a good relationship between the child and the other parent.

The real difficulty comes if you find she is telling the truth, or if you are just not sure. The law presumes that a parent who was physically abused by the other parent should have sole parental authority. Does Paul's evidence of his good character and deeds, stable job and good family overcome that presumption? If you rule in favor of Alice, and she is lying, you will have done a great injustice to Paul, and to his child. If you rule in favor of Paul and against Alice, and she is telling the truth, she will be devasted, and victimized all over again. And what does it say about the parenting abilities and character of a person who rapes another, then lies about it to gain an advantage?

There are no good answers here. You just have to do the best you can with what is presented. My thought is, assuming Alice is telling the truth, Paul did a horrible thing to her, and I can understand her position. But is it really in the child's best interest to never have a relationship with his father? There are plenty of situations in which one spouse does horrible things to the other—and why they don't stay together—but that doesn't necessarily mean that the child of the couple is better off without one of his parents in his life.

In the final analysis, we are supposed to be thinking of what is best for the child, not the parent. With all the other positives for Paul, it seems that it is in the child's best interests to figure some way for both parties to parent the child. If Alice wants to have no contact with Paul, that's understandable, and all communication can probably be worked through third parties. And there can be a gradual transition to have Paul enter the picture. Fortunately, I did not have to resolve the factual issues and rule in the case. The parties, with advice from their attorneys, reached an agreement—which was consistent with what I have suggested here.

Old Mother Hubbard

Kicked out of her shoe.

Assume you are a judge and are handling landlord tenant cases. On Christmas Eve, you receive a pro se motion from the mother of nine, who is the tenant in a case in which you entered a judgment for eviction a couple of days before, based on a default. "Pro se" means the person doesn't have an attorney. A "default" occurs when a defendant fails to file a response to a complaint within the time required by the rules of procedure. It's like when one player fails to show for a tennis match, he loses by forfeit and no match is played.

The motion says that she didn't understand that she had to file something in response, and that she would like to be heard at a hearing to explain her circumstances, i.e., that she lost her job and has not been able to find another. She asks to have until the first of the year to move out, so that maybe she can make arrangements for her and her children. Right now, she and the children have no place to go. You re-check the file and determine that all of the procedures required have been followed by the landlord. What do you do?

You could try to set up a quick phone conference hearing with both parties. Perhaps the landlord will agree to give the tenant extra time. It has been my experience that many plaintiffs in similar situations will agree. Of course, the tenant may not even have a phone, and even if she does, it will be difficult to get both on the phone before the end of the day. And what if you can get them by phone, and the landlord still insists on enforcing the judgment?

You could set the matter for a hearing a week later, which would, in effect, grant her motion, but that would be intellectually dishonest. On its face, the motion is legally insufficient. Inability to pay rent is not a defense to eviction.

You could just grant her motion without a hearing. The landlord won't like it, but probably very few others will find fault with you. Indeed, many people would consider this an appropriate bending of the rules on grounds of compassion. It is, however, an abuse of power, which is a dangerous, slippery slope to get on.

And what about the landlord? Isn't he entitled to have the law enforced? He did everything he was supposed to do, according to the law. He has bills too. He depends on the rental income to pay them. He needs to get another tenant in there as quickly as possible. Where is your compassion for him?

You could deny the motion but also try and put the tenant in touch with government human services agencies or local charities which may be of assistance. It's not exactly a judicial function, but there's no reason you can't act on your compassion, outside that official function.

Here we have another opportunity for you to evaluate where you are on the law versus justice, ends versus means continuum. You may see no conflict between law and justice or law and morality here. The judge should follow the law and deny the motion, and that will also be a fair result.

You may see no problem with finding a way to allow the tenant to stay, no matter that the law does not support it. If so, do you own it, acknowledge that you are disobeying the law?

Or do you do it on the sly, getting the result you want by abusing the process, denying the landlord his rights under the law?

For what it's worth, I think you appeal to the landlord's sense of compassion. In real life, I think the landlord would agree to a few extra days. It's Christmas Eve, for goodness sakes. It would take a hardened heart, indeed, to not grant this little bit of charity.

But it is the landlord's charity, not yours, to exercise. As a judge, you have a duty to uphold the law. No matter how bad you feel for the tenant, you can't just ignore the law. You can't just pick and choose when to follow it in your rulings. That is a clear route to arbitrariness. You may feel confident that you are doing the right thing, that you know where to stop along that slippery slope.

But do you? What if, with the holidays and an already crowded docket, you can't schedule a hearing for two weeks? Or a month? Do you still set the hearing? And if you just grant her motion without a hearing and give her additional days to move out, have you considered that this might make it more difficult for the landlord to find a new tenant if he can't show it until after the first of the month? Any way you slice it, you will have substituted your own judgment as to what is right and just for what the law requires. And as *Ox Bow* taught us, when you ignore the law while purportedly enforcing it, you make the law weaker.

So, I suggest that you deny her motion, perhaps expressing regret or sympathy for the tenant, and explaining in your order why you felt compelled to do so. Then, not as a judge but as a fellow human being, you try to help the tenant and her kids find other lodging and services. You probably have enough contacts and pull to help get something in place for her. Indeed, there is nothing stopping you from actively supporting, or even encouraging the forming of, a charity that is specifically aimed at helping persons like the tenant.

But that is just my perspective. The point is, reasonable people can disagree as to what is required, and whether justice results or not from whichever course is taken. Your answer to this, and the other hypotheticals should give you some real-life measure of your place on the ends-versus-means scale.

The 2020 Presidential Election and the January 6th Defendants

Stop the Steal. Two recent events in the real world dramatically illustrate this tension between ends and means. Specifically, they highlight three related themes in some of the films and stories we have looked at: that the courts are ineffective in handing out justice; that you may have to resort to self-help to get that justice; and that physical violence is an acceptable tool to obtain it.

The challenges to the 2020 presidential election results and the storming of the Capitol on January 6, 2021, are particularly compelling examples of this tension between just result and fair process. This is because of the very public nature of the cases and their scale of application. A sitting president who lost the election challenged the result by filing dozens of lawsuits in various courts. He lost in every instance, unable to prove his claims of fraud or other irregularities.

You would think that a person of such prominence, in fact, the leader of the country would, in such a situation, respect the process, would concede the election, and wish his opponent well going forward. Even if he really thought he was right and the multiple judges that considered the evidence and the applicable law were wrong, he would understand the message he would send by not doing so, i.e., that the process we rely on to resolve disputes fairly cannot be trusted.

But that was exactly what he did. The courts thus having proved to be ineffective in achieving a "just" result, this dissatisfied litigant resorted to self-help to get the "justice" he felt he was entitled to. He pressured state election officials to change their records to show him as the winner, to send alternative slates of electors to the electoral college. He pressured his vice president and members of congress to refuse to certify the results of the election.

Finally, having constantly repeated his unproven claims of a stolen election and stirred up his supporters, he urged them to come to Washington on January 6th. He spoke to the crowd assembled and urged them to march to the Capitol to fight for their country as they chanted "Stop the steal."

Now, you may argue that he did not advocate physical violence to "stop the steal" in his speech. But the fact is, the crowd, convinced by their leader's claims of a stolen election, of the injustice of it all, and the dire consequences for the country if the certification went forward, did become violent. And he did nothing to stop it for hours. So, you could also conclude that he condoned physical violence if it resulted in "justice" for him.

It didn't work. After some delay, the certification went forward. And many of those who stormed the capitol, assaulting law enforcement officers, damaging property, and disrupting the certification proceedings, were charged, tried, and convicted of various crimes. The January 6th defendants either pled to charges or were tried before juries who heard the evidence presented, applied the law to the facts, and rendered their verdicts. Some were sentenced to lengthy jail terms.

Fast forward to 2025, and the disgruntled litigant, having won election to the presidency, has pardoned, or commuted the sentences, of all of them. This blatant contempt for the process, in both the civil and criminal cases, is particularly damaging to our stability as an organized society because of who was involved. They were not friends or family of a defendant complaining about the result in a criminal case, nor some private victim of a crime deciding that the courts were ineffective in achieving justice and resorting to self-help. It was the President of the United States. And it was not just one case. We are talking about dozens of cases and dozens of defendants.

Nor was this a situation of a person frustrated by the failure of the courts to hold a person who violated the law accountable and impose a sufficient punishment. Just the opposite. This was an instance in which the most public figure in our country is essentially saying that the prosecutors, the judges, and the juries in our country cannot be trusted to achieve justice, and that physical violence in furtherance of getting what you decide is a fair result is okay. That is a most damaging and dangerous message from the leader of the country.

I am not oblivious to the fact that having a fair process does not always result in a fair result, but I think most of the time it does. I have not personally reviewed the evidence presented in any of these cases (nor, I am sure, have any of the critics of the results,) but I do know that each defendant had all the due process available to anyone charged with a crime, and the assistance of counsel. If there was a factual or legal defense available, I sure it would have been presented.

Some of you may say, well, the president has the authority to do that, and his predecessor pardoned lots of people, too. My response to that is two-fold. Just because you have the right to do something does not mean you should exercise that right. And pointing out that someone else has done something similar (assuming the acts are comparable) does not excuse your act. It is either morally right, fair, and just, or it is not.

That's my view. It may not be yours. But then you would be wrong. I'm kidding. Maybe. We all think we are right, don't we? And if we are, then people who disagree are wrong. I have family and friends who disagree with my perspective on this, who say that the actions of the president and his followers were justified to obtain justice. If any of them have gotten this far in the book, they will dismiss my observations out of hand. They don't want to hear it.

Indeed, many who become aware that there is a segment of this book critical of the sitting president, will refuse to read it and vocally attack it. Too bad. But then again, for anyone approaching the subject with a closed mind, this volume is not for you anyway.

My point is, an extreme results-oriented view of justice leads to arbitrariness. It is not conducive to a consistent, consensus-building approach to justice which binds us together. When we ignore the rules of procedure that have been established to determine the truth and administer justice accordingly, when we care only about getting the result we want, we weaken the rule of law to which we say we are committed.

Okay, down off my soapbox.

Looking back at these examples and analyzing your conclusions, do you want to replot yourself on the ends v means continuum? Trying to reach a workable balance between the two extremes, being as objective as possible, is the real challenge for us all.

So, what is the fair process that we balance against a fair result? What are those rules of procedure that have been established to determine the truth and administer justice? What seems to be working and what is not? What changes can we make to improve, to make it more likely to produce a fair and just result? The next section takes a stab at answering these questions.

IV

Framework for Justice: The Good, the Bad, and the Ugly

IN 1787, THE newly independent states adopted a constitution which gave to the central or national government certain enumerated powers with all other powers reserved to the states. This foundational, organic law set forth how the government was to be organized and how it would operate. Specifically, it created a legislative branch to make the laws, an executive branch to enforce the laws, and a judicial branch to interpret and apply the law to resolve disputes. The states have their own constitutions and state governments are similarly organized.

When we talk about the justice system, most people think of the judicial branch, the courts. But the product and actions of the other two branches are just as important to the goal of justice. So, in the big picture, when we talk about justice, the three branches are inextricably intertwined. We need to look at whether the laws themselves are fair, whether they are fairly enforced, and whether disputes are fairly resolved.

Substantive Due Process

Duly enacted laws: Are they constitutional? Are they fair?

I think most of us would agree that a duly enacted law can lead to an unfair or unjust result when applied. Martin Luther King, in his *Letters from a Birmingham Jail*, suggested that any law not rooted in "natural law" is not just, while any law that "uplifts human personality" is. And, he said, you further justice when you openly disobey an unjust law. Colonel Drummond in *Inherit the Wind* declared that "You can't fairly administer a wicked law."

Natural law is usually thought of as a body of unchanging moral principles regarded as a basis for all human conduct. Criminal laws are sometimes classified as malum in se, crimes that are naturally evil or wrong as adjudged by the sense of a civilized community. As the man in *The Ox Bow Incident* observed, "You just know things like murder and rustling are wrong." Other laws are considered malum per qua or malum prohibitum, those offenses that are wrong only because a statute makes it so, e.g., driving on a suspended license. In my opinion, the more we stick to the former and reduce the latter, the freer and the more just our society.

Enacted laws can be challenged as being contrary to the organic law of the country or state, i.e., as being unconstitutional. Most of the time the question is whether there is some rational basis for the law. Sometimes the challenge is that it is unfair as applied to a person or group. For example, a law that required all redheads to register for a military draft would probably be unconstitutional on both fronts – no rational basis for such a law and discriminatory against redheads in its application.

More Laws, Less Justice

Unlike such crimes as murder, assault, robbery and theft, there are some crimes, such as possession of certain substances (drugs) and gambling, in which there is no identifiable victim. The first question is why do we make something that does not harm anyone, other than oneself, a crime at all?

Part of it comes from a paternalistic tendency on the part of those in charge to decide certain things are not good for you. It is also in part an expansive view of who can be a victim. In some cases, the society at large is argued to be the victim. It is probably not worth spending a lot of time on it since, the fact is, they are crimes, but my view is that we should be very selective in making conduct that directly hurts no one other than oneself a crime. My libertarian streak, I suppose.

People will argue that drugs, for example, cause addictions, which cause people to steal and worse to support their habits. Similarly, people who develop a gambling habit or addiction will squander away money their family needs for food and shelter. No argument there, and if a person steals, he should be punished. But I would submit that the government should not be intervening in people's lives just because they engage in activity that isn't good for them with the rationalization that they may do something worse if they are not stopped. To me this is a public health issue, perhaps, an educational issue perhaps, but it shouldn't be a crime.

In my view, when you criminalize behavior that a large percentage of the population engages in, you weaken the law. And, in general, more laws, less justice. We live in a complex society and sometimes the law needs to reflect that. But the simpler, the better. Ignorance of the law may not be an excuse but when you need a lawyer to advise you what size fish and how many you can catch, you can understand how a person can unintentionally violate a law. I think that many times new laws are not necessary. The perceived problem can probably be addressed with existing law. It seems that legislators think that if they don't enact new laws, they're not doing their job. I think we'd all benefit from a culling of unnecessary laws and simplifying others.

You see, every time you change or add a law, it must be interpreted to be applied. That breeds lawsuits, and often unintended consequences, and always great expense. It uses resources that could have been used for core missions.

Now, I understand that our society is more complex than it was decades ago, and sometimes you need complex laws to address behavior not contemplated before. But, in general, the simpler you can make the law, the better. To the extent we can, our laws, especially our criminal laws, should be understandable to the ordinary citizen. And generally, the less law, the better.

Take the law against stealing, or theft. It makes sense, perhaps, to differentiate between theft of something of minimal value, petit theft, and theft of more valuable items, grand theft, although even this demarcation is arbitrary as to where you make the cut off. Aside from this, however, if you look in chapter 812 of the Florida Statutes, you will find a smorgasbord of variations on theft.

We have all sorts of distinctions, usually providing more severe punishment based on the value of what is taken or the nature of the property, or the owner, or the surrounding circumstances. For example, there are graduated penalties if property is valued at $5,000.00, $20,000.000, or $50,000.00, or $100,000.00, aggravated penalties for theft of an automobile, a semi-trailer, emergency medical equipment or law enforcement equipment, a will or codicil, a firearm, a farm animal, fire extinguisher, citrus fruit, items from a construction site, a stop sign, a controlled substance, any theft during a state of emergency, theft from a person 65 years age or older, farm produce, and failure to pay mass transit fee. These are not all of the variations, and it doesn't include the related crimes of being in possession of items to make theft easier, or dealing in stolen property, etc. Why do we need all these variations? Stealing is stealing. Can't we use common sense at the time of sentencing to differentiate as to what is more serious and deserving of harsher punishment?

Procedural Due Process

The Essentials – notice; an opportunity to be heard; a neutral arbiter

When we talk about due process, we mean the procedural requirements or rules that apply in the resolution of disputes, whether in criminal or civil cases, intended to provide a fair way to do so. The three essential elements of due process, regardless of the situation, are 1) notice, 2) an opportunity to be heard, and 3) a neutral arbiter of the dispute. The more serious the matter, the more formal the due process that is required. For example, a first-degree murder case has more procedural requirements than a case involving a misdemeanor charge, which in turn has more requirements than a case filed in small claims court.

The Decision to Arrest; the Decision to Charge

On the criminal side, law enforcement officers decide whether to arrest someone for a crime. Prosecutors decide whether to formally charge that person. There is a lot of discretion here and certainly room for abuse. The law offers some protection against arbitrary arrest. Specifically, the Fourth Amendment protects against "unreasonable searches and seizures." This usually means the law enforcement officer goes to a judge with an affidavit outlining the facts that give him or her reasonable grounds (probable cause) to believe the person has committed a crime. There are exceptions to the warrant requirement, but the officer still must have probable cause for the arrest and that determination is subject to later review by a judge.

Assuming probable cause is found, the prosecutor has great discretion in terms of whether and with what to charge, and what, if anything, to offer as disposition of the case. He or she is limited by an ethical duty not to go forward unless he or she has a good faith belief he or she can obtain a conviction.

Kafka's The Trial

In *The Trial*, Josef K., the chief clerk of a bank, is unexpectedly arrested by two agents from an unidentified agency for an unspecified crime. He is summoned to appear at the court's address the coming Sunday, without being told the exact time. He finds the court in the attic of a dilapidated working-class tenement block, at the back of a young washerwoman's home. Josef is rebuked for his lateness and is mistaken for a house painter rather than a bank clerk.

The following Sunday Josef goes to the courtroom again, but the court is not in session. He is never told what he is charged with. He becomes increasingly preoccupied by his case, to the detriment of his work. At the bank, one of Josef's clients recommends he seek the advice of Titorelli, the court's official painter. Titorelli outlines the options he can help Josef pursue: indefinite postponement of the process, or a temporary acquittal that could at any point result in re-arrest. Unequivocal acquittal is not a viable option.

On the eve of Josef's thirty-first birthday, two men arrive at his apartment. The three arrive at a small quarry outside the city, and the men kill Josef, stabbing him in the heart with a butcher's knife while strangling him. The absurdity of the story is in part because we find the lack of notice of the charge and an opportunity to defend against it, and to confront the witnesses against you, to be fundamentally unfair.

The Ox Bow Incident

When one of the suspected rustlers and murderers proclaims that "Even in this god-forsaken place we're entitled to a trial" he is told that "You're getting all the trial you're likely to get in this god-forsaken place as you call it. And the jury ain't too convinced."

In one sense there is due process to the extent that the men are told what they are accused of and an opportunity to be heard, though not much of one, certainly not the formality one would expect in a criminal case. But what is missing completely is the crucial requirement of a neutral arbiter to decide guilt or innocence, necessary for due or fair process.

As I write this, there is much public debate about the Trump administration's actions in picking up and sending individuals to a foreign prison who, it claims, are in the country illegally and have been determined to be gang members. So far Trump has defied a court order to "facilitate the return" of two of these specific individuals. In one of those cases, the administration admits that the person was removed in error.

Some people argue that the man is a criminal gang member or, at the very least, an illegal immigrant, not entitled to any due process. The fundamental problem with that is that our constitution says otherwise, i.e., that all *persons* have a right to due process before their liberty or property may be taken from them. And how do we know a person is a criminal gang member or is here illegally? Because the president or someone in the executive branch says he is? Is social media the place to present evidence and resolve the issue? No, due process requires at a minimum notice of the charge and an opportunity to confront the witnesses or evidence against you, with a neutral arbiter deciding the outcome.

If you rely on the representation of the executive in such matters, none of us are safe from arbitrary action. You could be picked up and transported to a foreign prison, the government claiming you are here illegally. But no, you say, I'm an American citizen, entitled to due process. But how do we know you are a citizen if there is no fair process to determine the issue, if the executive gets to decide?

The Adversary System

Both in the civil and criminal arena, our court system is in essence what we call an adversary system. The idea is that two skilled advocates on opposing sides advance their respective positions with evidence and legal argument, and that a neutral, objective arbiter—judge and/or jury—decide what the true facts are and the legal result. That's the ideal, but not always.

And Justice for All

A fundamental problem with the adversary system is stated by Al Pacino's character in the film, *And Justice for All*. Pacino plays criminal defense attorney, Arthur Kirkland, who is coerced into taking the case of a judge accused of rape. He doesn't like this judge. Neither do we, as we can see from his treatment of defendants and others, he is a real arrogant asshole. But Kirkland is a very good lawyer and the judge wants him, and he owes the other judge who tells him to take the case. The following are excerpts from one of the best opening statements in film history:

I am the defense counsellor for the defendant - Judge Henry T. Fleming. That man over there is the prosecuting attorney. And he couldn't be happier today. He is a happy man because today he's going after a judge. And if he gets him - he's gonna be a star. He will have his name in this month's Law Review, centerfold. Lawyer of the month.

Now, in order to win this case, he needs you. Naturally. You're all he's got. So, he's counting on tapping that emotion in you, which says: "Let's get somebody in power. Let's get a judge." However, these proceedings are here to see that justice is done. And justice is, as any reasonable person would tell you, finding the truth. And what is the truth today? One tragic truth - - is that that girl has been beaten and raped. Another truth is that the prosecution has no witness. Does not have one piece of evidence - - other than the testimony of the victim herself. Another truth is that my client voluntarily, - - and the prosecution is well aware of this, - took a lie detector test...

The prosecutor objects and the judge sustains it and tells the jury to disregard it. He explains that polygraph tests have not been proven reliable enough. They are inadmissible.

Sorry, Your Honor, Arthur says. *Let's get back to justice. What is justice? What is the intention of justice? The intention is to prove guilty the guilty and free the innocent. Simple, isn't it?.... Justice for all. Only we have a problem here. And do you know what it is? Both sides want to win. We want to win. We want to win regardless of the truth. We want to win regardless of justice. Regardless of who's guilty or innocent. Winning is everything.*

Arthur then repeats that the prosecutor has no evidence other than the testimony of the alleged victim. He says he has character witnesses and testimonials lined up from there to Washington D.C. and again makes reference to a lie detector test—which prompts another objection and a half-hearted apology from Arthur. Then he delivers the coup de grace.

The one thing that bothered me... The one thing that stayed in my mind and haunted me - was why? Why would she lie? What was her motive for lying? If my client is innocent, she's lying. Why? Was it blackmail? No. Was it jealousy? No. Yesterday I found out why. She doesn't have a motive. You know why? Because she's not lying. And ladies and gentlemen of the jury... The prosecution is not going to get that man today. No. Because I'm gonna get him. My client, the Honorable Henry T. Fleming, should go right to f... ing jail! The son of a bitch is guilty!.... If he's allowed to go free - - then something is really wrong here.

This is so satisfying because we have seen in previous scenes what a despicable character this judge is. And you know that every criminal defense attorney at some point, with some client, would love to deliver a similar opening statement. The problem, of course, is that it would be a flagrant violation of their duty to their client. Which it is here, as well. Arthur is hauled out of the courtroom, still arguing to the jury his client's guilt. He will be held in contempt and there will be a mistrial, so he has accomplished nothing other than the emotional release it afforded him, and the entertainment for us.

The winning-is-everything approach Pacino's character laments in the scene is something that runs through our society in everything from sports, to business, to politics, despite protestations to the contrary. We are a capitalistic society that thrives on competition. We compete for everything. We love contests, and we love a winner. "It's not whether you win or lose but how you play the game" is a saying for losers, according to many. To be sure, we say that we don't condone cheating or other misconduct in order to win, but the pressure to win is very strong. And while it sullies sports and business, it is a real danger when the end goal is justice.

The rules of procedure and the rules of professional conduct are designed to minimize, if not eliminate, the win-at-all cost mentality, but you can't help it sometimes.

I think most of us realize that the competitive spirit has to have limitations on occasion to serve an important value or principle. We want to win, but we want to win fairly. We depend on this sentiment to defend against the win-at-all cost attitude Pacino's character talked about.

My Cousin Vinny

If the idea behind the adversary system is that two advocates are pitted against each other and truth comes out in the middle, what do you do when the two advocates are not equal. You probably remember the scene from *My Cousin Vinny*, where the public defender gets up to do his opening statement, swaggers confidently over to the jury box, then proceeds to stutter his way through a short and useless opening statement, spraying spittle on jurors as he goes along. "I get a little nervous," he explains to his client as he sits back down. "I'm getting better."

The point is, the advocates for the parties come in various levels of skill. They are not all equal and the party with the more skilled attorney has an advantage. In my experience, that inequality does not necessarily mean that the client with the more skilled attorney will prevail. I mean, you can only do so much with what you have. If the evidence is stacked against you, and that evidence gets to the jury, they will figure it out.

I think we don't give jurors enough credit in that regard. Despite the uneven advocacy in a trial, jurors are not so shallow as to simply go with who makes the best argument. I think they generally do their best to analyze the evidence and apply the law to reach a proper verdict. I may not always agree with the verdict, but most of the time I do, and I almost always think they have taken their duty seriously and tried to follow the law to reach their verdict. Still, the ability of the attorney to marshal the evidence, effectively cross examine the witnesses for the opposing sides, and make a compelling argument, must be an important factor in any legal contest, and the party with the more skilled advocate has an advantage.

What about Atticus Finch's pronouncement in *To Kill a Mockingbird* that our courts are the great levelers? A fundamental principle or value of our justice system is that we are all equal before the law. No one is above the law and everyone is entitled to its protection. But he also realized that "people have a way of carrying their resentments right into a jury box".

I think both of those observations are true. We pride ourselves on being a country of laws, not men, and that all are equal before the law. It is an ideal not always realized, but that doesn't mean it's not a worthy ideal to pursue.

Plea Bargaining

To resolve the volume of cases that are filed each year, we depend on plea bargaining to resolve cases. The more trials, the more the backlog, and as they say, justice delayed is justice denied. On a theoretical level, we can argue that plea bargaining in general is a bad idea. It demeans the crime, and as a result, the victim, to bargain for a sentence, like a seller and buyer haggling in the bazaar. If a person commits a crime, he should be given a punishment that fits his crime. If he didn't do the crime, he shouldn't have been charged, and a jury should set him free.

The reality, though, is that things are not usually as black and white as we would like to think, or as is often portrayed in television shows, films, and literature. Both the prosecutor and the defense must factor into their decision the likelihood of success at trial and the likely sentence a judge might impose on a guilty verdict or a straight-up plea.

A word about the different pleas: A guilty plea and a not guilty plea are self-explanatory. You either admit or deny that you did what you are accused of. A plea of no contest, or nolo contendere if you want to show off your Latin, says that you are not admitting it, but you are not denying it either. You are just not going to fight it, to contest the charge at trial. A "straight-up plea" means there is no plea agreement and the defendant is prepared to take his chances with the judge as to sentencing.

For very practical reasons, most people chose to plead no contest rather than guilty to resolve a case short of trial. Both pleas subject you to the same punishment, i.e., the judge can adjudicate you guilty under either plea and impose an appropriate sentence. But a no contest plea does not admit guilt and thus cannot be used against you in a civil proceeding, for example. You can say that it was a plea of convenience. You didn't really do the crime, but given the sentence agreed upon, it was the better option. It was in your best interest.

This is one of the complaints about our current system of plea bargaining, especially as it applies to poor people who cannot make any reasonable bail and sit in jail awaiting trial or some other resolution of their case. At some point, they have been in jail so long they are willing to enter a plea to something they didn't do just to get out of jail.

It's a difficult issue, as the flip side of the argument is that some of these people are accused of serious crimes and there is a real concern that they will not appear back in court, or that they will continue to violate the law if they are released. And, if they were arrested, a judge had to determine there was at least probable cause to believe they did what they are charged with. Suffice it to say that plea bargaining is perhaps a necessary evil that gives us a form of rough justice. If not a perfect result, it is one both sides consider acceptable.

Certain crimes, under certain circumstances, by law result in mandatory minimum sentences if convicted. For example, in Florida, if you commit a certain type of crime within three years of your release from prison, your sentence will be automatically enhanced. You are labeled a Prison Releasee Reoffender. If you use a firearm in the commission of a crime, your sentence is enhanced. If you commit sexual battery on a child who is twelve years old or less you get a mandatory life sentence.

These statutes take away any discretion a judge might have as to sentencing, and puts the control in the hands of a prosecutor. Unless the prosecutor agrees to a lesser crime, there is little incentive for a defendant to enter a plea of guilty or no contest to the crime as charged and hope for a lesser sentence from the judge. This is because the penalty is the same whether he is found guilty by a jury after trial or pleads to it. At least with a trial you have a chance of a not guilty verdict, or one for a lesser charge. In other words, unless the prosecutor offers something less than as charged, the defendant has nothing to lose by going to trial. This, of course, increases the back-log of cases awaiting trial.

Neutral Arbiters – Judges and Juries

One of the essential components of procedural due process is a neutral arbiter to decide the case and resolve the dispute. From the beginning of a case until its final resolution, there will be disputes about the law or facts, usually both. Has the plaintiff stated a legally cognizable claim? Has the prosecution given sufficient notice of what it alleges the defendant did that was a crime? What information or documents must the opposing party share? What evidence may be presented during trial?

These are just a few examples of the disputes that may arise as a case moves forward. The resolution of these disputes is generally in the hands of a judge or a quasi-judicial office, e.g., a magistrate or hearing officer. If an appeal is taken, the question of whether the trial judge was legally correct in his rulings is decided by the appellate court, a panel of judges. The ultimate decision of whether the government has proven its charge in a criminal case or whether the plaintiff has proven his in a civil case is often in the hands of a jury.

In all these instances of decision-making, it is essential for due process, for fairness, that they be decided by someone who is neutral and objective. Giving someone notice and an opportunity to confront the evidence against him and to present a defense means little if the decision-maker cannot be not impartial. There are legal and practical safeguards in place that are intended to ensure that impartiality. Sometimes they work. Sometimes they don't.

Judicial Independence and Accountability

Miracle on 34th Street

In one of my favorite Christmas movies, *Miracle on 34th Street,* a man who claims to be the real Santa Claus, is subjected to a proceeding to determine if he is mentally ill and should be involuntarily committed for treatment. The district attorney prosecuting the case wants the judge to cut to the chase and rule that there is no Santa Claus.

Before the judge can rule, however, a man in the audience gets his attention and the judge takes a break. The man, played by William Frawley, (Fred Mertz on *I Love Lucy*) is your stereotypical political hack, complete with the cigar as a prop. He warns the judge that if he rules there is no Santa Claus, he's going to be very unpopular with a lot of people and groups. He tells him he will get just two votes in the next election, "yours and that district attorney out there." The judge shakes his head no and says, "The district attorney is a Republican."

Elected judges are aware that they may make rulings that will be unpopular. They are aware that following the law and doing what they think is right could result in losing their job in the next election. And most of them really like the job. So, there is a built-in concern that elected judges might forsake their objectivity in order to remain in their position. We worry that politics, ideology, or public opinion, might color the rulings of some elected judges on some occasions, especially in controversial, high-profile cases.

To counter this, we have to depend on two things: the integrity of judges and the buy-in by the public of the value of judges being independent in their decisions, and not being affected by personal feelings, or ideology, or by external pressure from the governor or the legislature, or from impassioned groups.

As one of my colleagues noted, "You have to love this job enough to lose it." Judges must have the courage to do the right thing and accept the consequences. There are things judges can do to minimize the negative consequences of rulings. For example, a judge can and should explain their rulings. It won't always work and not with everyone, for sure, but when people can understand how the judge got to his or her conclusion, that there is logic and reason behind it, most people will accept it, even if they don't agree with the ruling, because it comes from a good faith attempt to reach the correct conclusion.

And we must depend on the civic-minded public to do just that. We want judges to be objective and impartial. We need them to be so. We must depend on the appreciation of this fundamental concept by the majority of citizens. It is a principle that is constantly under attack, from politicians and special interest groups who are frustrated by court decisions. We must constantly resist and defend against these attacks—because we need confidence and trust in the integrity of judges and the system we have for resolving disputes, as imperfect as it may be. An independent judiciary is the one thing that sets us apart from other less free societies. It is the strongest protection against government overreach and attacks from any corner on our liberties.

One of the complaints against King George in the Declaration of Independence was that he had made judges dependent on his good will for their position and compensation. That is one of the reasons the founding fathers decided to have judges appointed for life. No independence issues there but it brings its own problem, as illustrated by the story of the three physicians who died and were at the gates of heaven, seeking entrance. The guard explains that entrance will be allowed based upon whether their services are needed in heaven at the time. So, he asks the first man what his specialty is.

"I'm an orthopedic surgeon," the man says.

"Gosh, I'm sorry but we have no broken bones here so we can't use you at this time."

So, this doctor walks away and the guard turns to the second one. "What is your specialty?"

He smiles. "I'm a pediatrician."

"Oh, I'm sorry, but all our children are happy and healthy, so we can't use you at this time."

He walks away and the third doctors starts to walk away as well. The guards asks, "Where are you going?"

He says, "Well, if you don't need them, I'm sure you don't need me, either."

"What is your specialty?"

"I'm a psychiatrist."

"Oh, yeah, we can use you. It's God. He thinks he's a federal judge."

The two rather humorous examples above point up the essential issue at the heart of the debate about elected versus appointed judges. There are two competing values at work here. Consider this question:

With which of the following statements do you most agree?

A. It is crucial that a judge be independent in order to be seen as impartial.

B. Accountability of a judge to the people is essential in a democracy.

As with the ends v means exercise we did earlier, I suspect most of you would agree with both statements, and the real question is, how do we achieve both without jeopardizing either? How do we balance them? An elected judge will tend to be more accountable, and an appointed judge will tend to be more independent. I think there are advantages and disadvantages to each method.

A judge is supposed to be non-political, so running in a partisan election is completely contrary to that notion, and I think a bad idea. Even in a non-partisan election, there is at least the appearance of political influences and debts. There is pressure to appeal to certain political bases, with a resultant expectation of how the judge will rule in the future. Because of the restrictions in the judicial canons, however, candidates are severely limited in what they can say or do. Basically, you promise to be fair, tout your experience and dedication, and hope for the best. You are not allowed to even hint at how you might rule in certain cases, or even what your position is on certain hot political issues.

In such a restrictive world, how is the voter supposed to know who to vote for? How can they effectively evaluate the candidates? In a small or medium-sized community, word-of-mouth can be effective. The local lawyers will have some experience with or be aware of how each candidate is regarded in the legal community. The candidates will have left impressions on others in the community at large, as well. It's not perfect, but the chances of the voters knowing enough about the candidate to make an informed decision are good.

In a large community, like Miami, or Tampa, or Orlando, word-of-mouth is less effective. The bar is so large that many lawyers will not have had the opportunity to get to know the candidates. Thus, while some bar associations conduct polls, which are of some use, the sample of lawyers drawn may be too small, or not sufficiently objective, Thus, voters have less of a chance to know about, and evaluate, candidates for judicial positions.

In the larger counties, then, appointment may seem to be the better route. The argument for appointment is that it takes the politics out of it. Candidates are not required to raise money, nor seek support from political leaders to get elected. The counter-argument is that you have not taken politics out of it but rather given the power to decide to a smaller circle of politically connected persons. True, the appointment process is still political, and many very qualified persons do not even apply if they are of the wrong party, i.e., one different than that of the governor.

But at least with a judicial nominating commission (JNC) screening the applicants, as we have in Florida, you have some assurance that whoever is selected will be qualified. The JNCs, instituted during Ruebin Askew's term as governor, were a great innovation and a safeguard against incompetent, corrupt or ideological political hacks taking the bench. Three members of the JNC were appointed by the governor, three by the President of the Florida Bar, and those six would select three from the public at large. The commission interviews the candidates, researches them, and recommends to the governor 3-6 names.

You don't necessarily have that in an election.

Unfortunately, this system was weakened during Jeb Bush's term as governor. Now the governor makes all appointments, which makes it less likely that the JNC will exercise independent judgment. Still, you have a review of the candidates and an evaluation by a group with access to more information than the public might have.

In the federal system, there is even less restraint. There is no equivalent to the JNC to limit who a president may appoint, including to the Supreme Court. The president nominates and the senate confirms the appointments. Now, there may be contentious hearings in the senate, but very rarely is the person not confirmed.

So, what's the safety valve against the arrogance that comes with an appointment for life? How do we guard against the danger that the judge will be a political hack with an agenda at worse, or at best, less than impartial in approaching his or her duties? On the independence versus accountability scale, the scale tips heavily in favor of independence for the appointed judge. So, something must counter this to give them some accountability for their rulings. How do we do that? A federal judge can be impeached and removed from office, but not very easily. That is by design. And it has very rarely occurred.

My thought is that no matter who appoints them, whether they are considered liberal or conservative by those who care about such things, we must believe, and I do, that they want to do a good job, and be considered a good judge. They want to be highly regarded by their peers. Just as we must depend on the integrity of elected judges not to bow to political pressure, we must depend on the integrity of appointed judges to exercise good faith in interpreting and applying the law, regardless of their personal feelings or desires.

We must depend on the judge's peers to reign in those who violate the trust we place in them to be impartial and objective. We also must depend on the Senate to exercise some degree of control and keep out appointees who are clearly unqualified or beyond the pale as to political leanings.

In the final analysis, regardless of the method of selection, we want judges who will uphold the constitution, will do their best to set aside personal feelings or outside pressures, will treat people with respect and courtesy and listen to both sides, and who will apply the law in good faith to the facts as found by evidence in making their judgments. And that depends on us. As citizens, we must understand that it is in everyone's best interest, regardless of political affiliation, to seek and retain judges who will perform in this manner. We should insist on it. We must look to long-term stability rather than short-term political gain. We must be committed to these values and vigorously fight all attacks on them as the danger to the republic they are.

Well, I hope we've cleared up that whole elected versus appointed question.

Impartiality

One of the key elements or components of our justice system is having a neutral, objective person or persons deciding the case. Anything that gives the appearance of partiality or a lack of objectivity lessens the trust in the justness or fairness of the outcome. A judge is required to remove herself from a case (recuse) if she feels she can't be impartial. A litigant can move to disqualify a judge if she has good reason to believe the judge will not be fair.

One of the judicial canons governing judicial conduct concerns avoiding statements or actions that suggest a judge does not keep an open mind on any case that comes before him or her. It can be aggravating when you are attacked in the press and can't answer. You must depend on lawyers or others to come to your defense. But you can see why the rules are there. It's very important. And there are plenty of stages of a case in which a judge needs to be careful in this regard.

The Rainmaker

In the film, *The Rainmaker,* Matt Damon's character, Rudy, is suing an insurance company for wrongfully denying a claim by his client. At the pretrial conference, when opposing counsel excuses himself to go to the restroom—what appears to have been planned—the judge tells Rudy that he's not impressed with the merits of his case and is considering dismissing it. But, he says, maybe he can lean on Leo (the opposing attorney) to come up with some money.

Rudy tells him that Leo has offered him $75,000.

"Seventy-five thousand?" the judge says, disbelief in his voice. "Well, that's a lot of money. Jeez, you'd have to be crazy to turn that down."

Here the judge gives the impression that he doesn't want the case "clogging up his docket." He is advocating a settlement proposed by opposing counsel. On top of the apparent collusion between counsel and judge, it leaves the impression that the judge is less than neutral and that if the case proceeds to trial, Rudy will be at a disadvantage.

The Verdict

In *The Verdict*, Paul Newman's character is a lawyer suing doctors and a hospital for medical negligence. In the middle of his examination of his expert witness, the judge interrupts to ask the witness a question.

"Are you saying that the failure to restore a heartbeat was in itself negligent?" When Newman objects, the judge insists that he has the right to ask the witness a "direct question." He says "Let's not waste these people's (jury) time."

When the judge repeats the question, the witness says that, given the limited context of his question he would have to say no. The judge, who is standing now, confirms, "Then you're saying the doctors were not negligent?"

Newman then tells the judge, "If you're going to try my case, try not to lose it."

The rules do allow a judge to ask questions of witnesses but it should be done infrequently and always in a neutral manner. Never in a manner resembling cross-examination. Now, this is drama and not real life. I can't imagine a judge ever coming close to something like that in a jury trial. Of course, in a non-jury trial, you might ask more questions because you are the fact-finder. You want to make the right decision based on all the pertinent facts. If something seems inconsistent, you want to see if there is an explanation. But even in a non-jury trial you must be careful not to suggest a pre-conceived notion in your questioning, not to cross-examine witnesses. It suggests that you are not neutral or impartial. And this mask of impartiality is essential to promoting confidence that the procedure is fair.

This "mask of impartiality" must be worn off the bench as well as on it. You are a judge 24/7 and everywhere you go. This means you don't comment publicly on any controversial topic that might end up in court. You are a judge. You don't have an opinion, at least not publicly. You don't endorse political candidates or give them money or put their signs in your yard. You shy away from anything political.

It also means you can't appear to be too close to the lawyers who appear before you, or beholden to them in any way. For example, suppose a lawyer offers you tickets to a basketball game. Even if you pay for it and you are seen sitting in their box, people may see you together and draw the wrong conclusion. You don't talk to one side of a case without the other side being there or copied on written correspondence.

And try as you might, you, like everyone else, have your biases, your way of looking at things that come out without you really knowing it. You may be perceived by others as leaning one way or the other, for example, in criminal cases. It's helpful to ask yourself which side in criminal cases is most pleased to have you preside? You hope the answer is both, but you should be constantly monitoring it.

It's also important to monitor your verbal and non-verbal communications as a judge. Studies suggest that jurors are looking at the judge for some clue as to how they should find, even though the judge assures them that he has no interest in how the case should be decided. A judge's facial expressions and body language may be sending unintended messages.

Changing Lanes

Disrespect can be intentional, as when the judge in *And Justice For All* tells a defendant that he is" a disgusting scum of the earth who should be taken out and squashed like a bug." It can also be unconscious, though, too. A scene from the film, *Changing Lanes*, illustrates this well.

The character played by Samuel L. Jackson is in an accident on the way to court and thus is late to the hearing on his ex-wife's request to move with the children to another state. When he gets there, the hearing is just concluding, and his ex-wife and her attorney are leaving the courtroom. When Jackson tries to explain why he is late, the judge is dismissive, telling him that "if it was my hearing, I'd be on time" pointing out that everybody else managed to be on time.

The judge allows Jackson to read a statement he has prepared about how boys need their fathers and how he is in the process of getting a house. "It's not much, but I can fix it up." All the time Jackson is giving his impassioned speech, the judge is looking at and signing papers on his desk, then he patronizes the man by telling him to keep his eyes on the prize, so to speak, and sends him on his way. The perception here is that the judge is too busy to give this man his attention, and that the man's concerns are not worthy of consideration.

First, if the judge is going to hear from him at all, he shouldn't let the other side leave. That's ex parte communication, i.e., having communication with one side of a case without the other side being present or copied on the communication. This is not allowed under the judicial canons of ethics. It signals that nothing the man says will make a difference.

And he should listen to him. Yes, it's irritating when people are late, which can be a sign of disrespect to the other side and the judge, but there may be a good reason, as here. And even if not, best to throw your schedule off a bit and listen to what the man has to say, address his arguments and then rule. Otherwise, the man feels, rightly, that the judge is just punishing him for being late instead of seeking what is in the best interests of the children.

Selecting a Fair and Impartial Jury

My Cousin Vinny

You may remember the jury selection scene in this movie in which the prosecutor asks a juror how she feels about the death penalty. She replies that she thinks that should be left to the victim's family. The prosecutor then starts describing the heinous nature of the murder in this case and before he can finish, she interrupts and says "Fry 'em."

In Florida, and in most states I imagine, jurors in a case are selected in a process by which the judge and the parties ask questions of potential jurors to weed out those who can't be fair and impartial in serving as a juror. This selection process is sometimes called voir dire – a French term meaning to see and to hear. After questioning, each side can ask the judge to excuse any juror "for cause" if their answers suggest an inability to be fair and impartial. They have an unlimited number of "cause" challenges.

They also have a certain number of "peremptory" challenges. These can be exercised for any reason -- except discriminatory ones based on race or disability, for example. The lawyer might just have a feeling about the prospective juror but not enough to challenge for cause.

The process is intended to pick a jury that can decide the case on the evidence presented and the law as the judge instructs them, and not because of some preconceived notions or feelings. It's not perfect, but from my experience, I think it works for the most part. I believe jurors take their oath seriously and are very conscientious in trying to do the right thing. Not always, but most of the time. And we depend on that conscientiousness to make it work.

Creative Jury Service Dodges

In Gadsden County, I was picking a jury one time and a man asks to be excused as he was a sole proprietor of a business. I was sympathetic but he did have employees so it was more an inconvenience than a real hardship, and there were many people in that same situation who had not been excused. So, I denied his request. Later, as we moved through questioning of the potential jurors, this same man asked if he could "approach the bench" to tell me something.

I said okay and had the lawyers come up, too. At the bench, the man said, "Judge, I am from southwest Louisiana, Cajun country."

"Yes."

"In Cajun country, growing up, there was always someone in the neighborhood who was a shine."

"A shine? What's a shine?""

"Yeah, a shine is a person who can see the future and can see auras around people."

"Oh," I said.

"Yeah, and in my neighborhood, I was the shine."

"Oh," I said again, and the lawyers are rolling their eyes by now.

"Yeah," the man said again. "And I have to tell you, I've been sitting here all morning, looking at the defendant over there." He chances a quick look in the direction of defense counsel table. "And the man has a dark, dark aura all around him. I don't think I can be fair to him."

More eye rolling.

"And in contrast, Judge, your aura is a nice golden hue, calm and tranquil."

The eyes were really rolling now, and snickers no doubt stifled, including my own.

"Well, thank you for this new information, Mr. Smith. I'm sure it will be helpful to the attorneys in making their decision. Go ahead and take your seat again."

He got this surprised look on his face, like he thought he would be let go right then, but he went back to his seat. I told the lawyers, "That was easily the most creative excuse to get out of jury duty I've heard, and it's obvious he's not going to be picked." The lawyers nodded. "But I say we let him sit here till we pick a jury." The heads nodded again.

We concluded the voir dire, selected a jury, and dismissed the remaining jurors, including Mr. Shine from Cajun country. Now, I don't know if I misheard the guy or if I spelled shine correctly but a google search I did later yielded nothing to corroborate the guy's story. But as I said, it was pretty darn creative. Perhaps I should have let him go just for that, but it didn't seem fair to the other people who were having to sacrifice their time and were taking their civic duty seriously.

Respect and Courtesy

Early on we talked about the opening scene from *The Godfather* and the importance of respect as bearing on our perception of whether we received justice. People like to see Judge Judy rip into a litigant, but I guarantee you the litigant doesn't like it. Everybody, and I mean everybody, deserves to be treated with respect, to be allowed their dignity. That doesn't mean that we should tolerate bad behavior or disrespect from those in court. That must be dealt with, but we should never let someone else's conduct determine what sort of person we are.

Inherit the Wind

For some judges and others in the system, respect is a one-way street, and woe unto the defendant or lawyer or other participant who fails to show it. The ultimate sanction for such disrespect is contempt of court, a criminal charge which a judge can utilize with very little due process if it is direct contempt.

Direct contempt means it happens in front of the judge. Indirect contempt means it happens outside of court where the judge only learns of it through others. In the latter, the judge conducts a hearing after due notice, takes testimony and decides if the accused has willfully refused to abide by a court order. In direct contempt, the judge gives the offending person an opportunity to show cause why they shouldn't be held in contempt of court for their inappropriate and disrespectful behavior. If the judge is not satisfied, he or she can find the person in contempt and sentence them on the spot.

A good example of this contempt power occurs in the film, *Inherit the Wind*, which involves the Scopes monkey trial. A teacher in Tennessee is prosecuted for teaching evolution in his class. A frustrated defense attorney, played by Spencer Tracy, suggests that his client can't get a fair trial in this bigoted community. When asked what reasons he has for his conclusion, he points to the audience and says something to the effect that there are a hundred reasons. "And if that's not enough," he says, "there's one more," he says looking back to the judge.

The judge gives him a stern look and says, "I hope counsel does not mean to imply that this court is bigoted."

The lawyer replies, "Well, you have the right to hope."

As you can imagine, it goes downhill from there and the judge ends up holding the lawyer in contempt, and imposing a fine of $2000, which was a lot of money back then. When the lawyer gives a sarcastic reply, "Why don't you make it $4000," the judge says, "It's $4000."

My Cousin Vinny

One of the most well-known, and funniest, scenes of a lawyer being held in contempt is the arraignment scene in *My Cousin Vinny*. Fred Gwynn, perfectly cast as an Alabama trial judge, deals with the clueless attorney from New Jersey, Vincent Gambino, played by Joe Pesci. At the arraignment of his clients on a charge of murder, the judge chastises Vinny for not standing when addressing the judge, and for his inappropriate clothes—leather jacket. "Next time you appear in my court, you will look lawyerly. And I mean you'll comb your hair and wear a suit and tie. And that suit better be made of some kind of... cloth."

The final straw comes when the judge tries to get him to enter a plea to the charge and Vinny keeps trying to explain that it was all a misunderstanding. "I don't need explanations," the judge patiently explains. "All I need is a simple answer to a simple question." He tells him what he wants to hear is either guilty or not guilty. "If I hear anything other than guilty or not guilty, you will be in contempt. I don't even want to hear you clear your throat. Now, I think I have been clear." Then, with exaggerated slowness, he says, "How do your clients plea?"

Vinny can't help himself. He says, "I think I get the point."

"No," the judge says, "I don't think you do." Then he proceeds to hold Vinny in contempt.

It's a very funny fish-out-of-the-water scene, but was the judge justified in holding the lawyer in contempt? There were other, less drastic measures he could have taken, but it wouldn't have been nearly as entertaining. He could have taken Vinny aside and explained the local customs and requirements in his courtroom instead of embarrassing him in front of everyone. But all things considered, I think the judge gave him plenty of chances and warned him explicitly as to what would happen if he uttered anything other than guilty or not guilty. I wouldn't be Monday morning quarterbacking this one.

One of the first training and educational courses Florida judges take upon entering office is on the law of contempt. Judges are cautioned against using this tool, the suggestion being that it is a sign that you have lost control. There are indeed many ways short of contempt by which a judge can handle inappropriate behavior, and I agree that that is the best course.

A lot of times, the inappropriate behavior is a result of heightene d emotions, said in the heat of battle, so to speak. Once things settle down, the person realizes this and will apologize.

One option in this situation is to call a recess and let tempers cool down, then confer with the lawyers privately. Explain that such comments are not to be tolerated and give the lawyer a chance to apologize when court resumes, accept the apology and move on.

When a lawyer was showing his butt, maybe with snide remarks about opposing counsel, or constantly interrupting me or counsel, I would sometimes channel Marlon Brando's *Godfather*. I'd wait until they had finished, give a long pause while they thought about it, then say in a soft, sad voice, "What have I ever done to make you treat me so disrespectfully?" This almost always worked, even with lawyers who weren't familiar with the source of the statement. They would apologize and promise to cease and desist such behavior.

Sometimes, in the heat of battle, the attorneys will begin to reply directly to a comment by opposing counsel. A tactic I sometimes used in this situation was to ask the other attorney how he or she ruled. When both attorneys looked at me in surprise, I would explain to the attorney that if he was going to make his argument to the other attorney, I would let the attorney rule on the motion. That always got an apology and a return to decorum.

A couple of times when the lawyers were arguing to each other instead of arguing their case to me, and things were getting really heated, I stood up and left the room, telling them that when they needed a judge to let me know. After a brief recess, both attorneys were apologetic and promised not to let it happen again, and we were able to proceed without further problems.

One of my colleagues, a thorough gentleman, would wait for the interrupting person to finish, then say, "I apologize for continuing to talk while you were interrupting me." These are examples of how the situation can be defused with humor, suggesting that the judge understands the person is upset and adding a contempt sentence is not worth the effort. You have to be careful with humor, though, as to some it may seem disrespectful, especially to the person who is the butt of the joke.

And Justice for All

One entertaining option to the contempt process in keeping order in the courtroom is from the film, *And Justice for All*, which we have talked about earlier. In one scene, Al Pacino's client, who is charged with illegal gambling, sneaks over to the prosecution table during a recess, and starts eating the lotto tickets that are the evidence against him. The prosecutor, alerted to the situation by the court reporter, with whom he is flirting, rushes over and grabs the defendant, trying to make him spit out the tickets. Pacino comes to his client's rescue and the court deputy gets involved and soon we have a general melee going on in the middle of the floor.

This is when the judge comes into the court through a side door. He sees the commotion, pulls a gun from a holster on his side and fires it into the ceiling. Not surprisingly, this gets everyone's attention, and they freeze, looking in the judge's direction. The judge, still holding the gun, says, "Gentlemen, may I remind you that you are in a court of law? Now, let's proceed in an orderly fashion."

Pretty funny, but not recommended. There have, in fact, been instances in Florida in which a judge has brandished or displayed a gun in court. It almost never ends well for the judge, not in terms of physical injury, but in being disciplined by the Supreme Court, including being removed from the bench.

The Godfather and Changing Lanes Revisited

But what about from the other side of the bench? As we discussed in *The Godfather*, the perception or feeling that we are being respected is an important component of justice. The essence of this is the feeling that you have been heard, that your argument has been considered.

You will remember the scene from Changing Lanes, discussed earlier, where the character played by Samuel L Jackson (the dad) is late to the hearing. He is allowed to give his side (after the judge has excused his wife and her counsel) but it's clear the judge is not really listening. He is not considering what the dad has to say, even though he is quite passionate about it. Rather, the judge is dismissive, disrespectful.

It is thus important for those who make decisions, including judges, to at least appear to be interested in what the litigants have to say. And just as importantly, when a decision is made, an effort should be made to explain the ruling in a way that demonstrates the litigants have been heard and their arguments considered. It is, to me, common courtesy, a sign of respect. It's not legally required, but it is an important element to promoting confidence and trust in the process. Even when a party disagrees, they can at least understand how the judge came to his or her decision. And so can the appellate court which may review the decision on appeal.

V

Just Results: Crime and Punishment

ASSUMING WE FOLLOW a fair process, and assuming a person is found guilty of a crime, how do we determine a fair and appropriate punishment? It is an ideal area for us to apply some of those general principles or components of justice we have looked at to specific facts and circumstances, and to real cases.

Express Purposes of Sentencing

Punishment, Deterrence, Incapacitation, Rehabilitation

Our laws on sentencing in Florida are collectively called The Punishment Code. The title gives it away, don't you think? It states that the primary purpose in imposing a sentence is punishment. The other express statutory purposes are reform and rehabilitation, deterrence, both individual and general, and incapacitation, but they are secondary to punishment.

But how do we know how much is the right amount of punishment? The Sentencing Guidelines give the judge a floor, but he or she can give up to the maximum statutory punishment without having to give a reason. And how do we balance punishment with the other expressed purposes of sentencing--reform and rehabilitation, deterrence, both individual and general, and incapacitation?

Some will say that the punishment should be sufficiently severe, but not greater than necessary, to accomplish its purpose? Well, yes, but how do you determine what is sufficient but not greater than necessary? I suggest that there are multiple factors you should consider, competing values and principles you must weigh and balance to arrive at what you conclude is the proper sentence in each case.

Different people will reach different conclusions. My expectation is that the differences will be a matter of degree, and within a reasonable range of each other. When the difference is broader and more fundamental, we should ask ourselves why and see if there are ways to bridge or narrow the gap.

Deterrence is an offshoot of punishment, both for the individual and the public. The harsher the sentence, the greater the deterrence—at least in theory. Any sentence that includes some period of incarceration necessarily includes a component of *incapacitation*. If that's all we are doing, though, we should be concerned with the social cost and risk of recidivism (re-offending) when the defendant is released.

There are some people, perhaps, who can't be rehabilitated, who should be put away as long as possible simply to protect the public from their menace. But we never know for sure who these people are. Except in rare cases, I think you should sentence a person, hopeful that he can successfully re-enter society.

The theory here is that in addition to punishing the offender, we are trying to "correct' his behavior so that he doesn't do it again. If so, it makes sense that we try to address the root causes of the behavior, try to give the person the knowledge, skills and treatment that will aid him in avoiding such conduct in the future. I remember a defense attorney telling me the story of a judge at sentencing telling a defendant that he was giving him a second chance. The defendant replied, "No, you are giving me the same chance over again."

On the other hand, why should the courts be involved in "social work"? Isn't that for the executive branch of government? Or the family, the church, or the individual? Does the imposition of conditions such as drug treatment, anger management, counseling, etc. diminish personal responsibility, and imply that the person has no incentive, no motivation, no responsibility to improve on his own? Does such a paternalistic approach foster dependency?

Mens Rea (Criminal Intent) vs. Harm Done

Mens rea is a Latin phrase that translates to "guilty mind" and refers to the mental state of a defendant accused of a crime. It is the intention or knowledge of wrongdoing that constitutes part of a crime, as opposed to the act itself. The extent of the bad intention is a factor most would consider in deciding on an appropriate sentence. So is the harm done to the victim. Sometimes, they are at odds with each other, i.e., the harm done is way out of proportion to the wrongful intention or mens rea, and vice versa.

DUI Manslaughter

In a DUI Manslaughter case, for example, the mens rea is knowingly getting behind the wheel after having consumed too many alcoholic drinks. Consider these two examples of mens rea but with starkly different results….

In the first, a person with a blood alcohol level three times the legal limit drives and is involved in an accident that is clearly his fault, but fortunately no one is hurt. Unless he has an extensive history, the defendant will likely receive a probationary sentence. No jail.

In the second, a person is driving with a blood alcohol level slightly above the legal limit. He is involved in an accident in which the other driver dies. The other driver was at fault and the primary cause of the accident, but the defendant also contributed to the accident. The defendant can thus be charged with DUI Manslaughter. If convicted, he will face a minimum sentence of several years in prison, regardless of his prior criminal history. The mens rea, or criminal intent, in the first scenario is much stronger than in the second but the punishment is much more severe in the second.

Another example of this dynamic is attempted murder versus murder. The mens rea or evil intent is present in both to the same degree. The only difference is that in one the defendant was unsuccessful. Should this person be rewarded with a lesser sentence for being a bad shot, or otherwise incompetent? Yet, that is what the law provides.

The only explanation for the different treatment is the harm done and the notion of balancing the scales. A life has been taken, regardless of the degree of mens rea or evil intent involved, and recompense must be made to somehow recover some sort of equilibrium. So, a punishment must sometimes balance the mens rea against the harm done.

A Father's Pain: A Judge's Duty

Consider this actual case from Utah. The information provided is from an article that appeared in the Los Angeles

Times on December 30, 2001, by Times staff writer, Barry Siegel.

On an October morning, high in a remote forest of Utah, Paul Wayment surveyed a rugged 8,000-foot-high hunting ground where deer and elk and moose wander through dense stands of golden aspens. Behind him, strapped in a car seat in his red Dodge pickup, sat his son, Gage. By all accounts, the man was a wonderful father. He and his toddler son, over whom he had sole custody, were inseparable. They did everything together. Camping and boating as often as they could. Playing ball in the backyard, fixing things around the house, planting their vegetable garden. Mr. Mom, the neighbors called him.

Wayment spotted five deer gliding into the forest. He began to follow them over a ridge. He walked a mile, maybe two. Then he began to have a bad feeling. He rushed back to the pickup and found the driver's side door wide open and Gage gone. Wayment, in a panic, set out in search of the toddler, even thrashing about in a nearby pond, but couldn't find the little boy. He called for help.

The first deputy sheriff to arrive found Wayment writhing on the ground, crying and vomiting, his face caked with snot and pond mud. "Just shoot me," Wayment urged when the deputy asked what he could do for him.

The boy was found two days later. Six inches of snow covered the small body. Gage lay in a fetal position, his hands clenched, his eyes wide open. His pajama legs were up to knees; his feet had worn through his thin booties. His throat was blue. In his eyes were frozen tears.

The prosecutor, Robert Adkins, agonized on whether, and with what, to charge the father. The deputies and detectives who had spent more time with him than anyone felt Wayment had already suffered enough. But Waymont had left Gage in a rugged, isolated area, with the pickup parked on a slant, which meant the car door could easily swing open, pulled by gravity. He had gone some unknowable length of time, anywhere from 30 to 90 minutes. Certainly, it was not OK to do what Wayment did. Still, this was clearly a good man who had made a horrible mistake. He was a straight arrow, in fact, who didn't drink or use drugs. He had no criminal history. To forgive and empathize, or condemn and punish?

In the end, Adkins decided to charge him with negligent homicide, a misdemeanor. He also decided he would not seek a jail sentence. He just couldn't argue for incarceration. Not in this situation, not where the man's son had died.

Wayment entered a no contest plea in exchange for the prosecutor's agreement not to seek incarceration. The local judge, Robert Hilder, told those gathered before him that he was not bound by the agreement for sentencing. He retained the right to impose jail or any other penalty. Wayment said he understood. The plea was accepted and a sentencing date set.

Hilder pondered for days about Paul Wayment. There was no need for deterrence here, and no need for punishment, but there had to be a consequence. There was a need for society to make a statement, for society to say, this is wrong. There was also a need for rehabilitation. Hilder felt Wayment must pay some kind of penance, or he would never be able to put this behind him. He imposed a 30-day jail sentence, allowing him to report to the jail the following morning.

Wayment never reported to the jail. They found his body on a sloping ridge next to a pair of binoculars, a Pepsi Big Gulp and a Winchester .243 hunting rifle. He'd picked a spot, surrounded by aspens, that provided a view of the hills where they'd searched for Gage, and then put a bullet through his head.

Hilder faced a barrage of criticism immediately after Wayment's death. A few particularly harassing letters prompted the county to provide temporary protection. Where once there were calls for accountability and consequences, now there was outrage at the judge who provided just that. People assailed Hilder, demanding his resignation or dismissal, charging him with "a pathetic lack of wisdom," declaring him "directly responsible for the death of Paul Wayment."

But soon enough, there came an even greater wave of support for Hilder from lawyers, pundits, hundreds of citizens and from Wayment's sister, Valerie Burke. "I don't believe the 30-day sentence caused Paul to kill himself," she told reporters. "I think the judge was compassionate. Our family understands where the judge was coming from, and we don't blame him at all. He had to do what he felt was right."

Hilder can only shake his head at that phrase, "what he felt was right." He takes comfort from all the support but is no more certain now than before of making correct decisions. This latest experience, above all, has made him look even harder at the role of the judge.

He reflects on what the law accomplishes, what the law can't accomplish. He loves the law but does not worship it. He believes it does not have the answer to everything. In matters full of ambiguity, he suggests there may be no good solution. "Black and white answers are not always what's needed," he says. "But sometimes they're the only answer." He says something else as well: "It's not a bad thing to have Paul Wayment's face forever part of my life."

This is a particularly poignant story and presents well the dilemma or conflicting values at work when you have great harm but little need for punishment. This is because the harm is to someone close to the defendant. The thing that makes this case so difficult is the obvious bond between father and son and the obvious mental torture the father endured, and his sincere remorse. Change the facts a little and those who argue that the man has suffered enough might change their minds.

For example, what if Gage was not his child, but rather a neighbor's child who he had agreed to watch over that afternoon? Or a daycare worker who decided to take a side trip to scout out a hunting area? What if he was portrayed as a rather careless and uninvolved parent, not the "Mr. Mom" his neighbors described? What if he had never been a great parent and wanted custody of his child so he didn't have to pay child support? What if he had complained that Gage was "cramping his style" with the ladies and that he often palmed him off to babysitters or relatives? I suspect that people would be much more likely to argue for harsher punishment.

Certainly, you have known or heard of cases in which parents do ridiculously stupid things that result in the death of their child: A child, not properly supervised, dies of heat stroke in a car, or drowns in the family pool, or falls to his death from an open window, or falls from the bed of a pick-up truck. The examples are unfortunately numerous. The mental pain to the negligent person is often quite profound, more punishing than anything we can do to them. We feel empathy for them, but we are also cognizant of the need to send a message to all parents and caregivers out there to please, please, think about what you are doing and be more careful with our children.

Hindsight is always 20/20, but do you agree with the judge's sentence? Why or why not? What do you think of his decision to make a public statement about the case—something that is rarely done? Did the statement affect your perception of whether he had done the right thing in sentencing Wayment? As the judge foresaw early on, there was no right answer. He would have to land somewhere, but whatever he did, there would be many people who disagreed.

I find no fault whatsoever in Judge Hilder's sentence in the case. He seems to be a caring, conscientious person who took his responsibility seriously and showed courage to go against the prevailing sentiment. And I don't think that was the cause of the man's suicide either. That being said, I probably would not have imposed any jail myself. I don't think it was necessary to send the message to others, as the judge reasoned. There was a consequence. The man lost his son and will live with a terrible guilt for the rest of his life. Some probation with community service would have been more productive, I think.

Accidental Shootings

I had a case in which a college student accidentally shot and killed his roommate, who was also his best friend since high school. On the day of the shooting, the defendant and the victim were working on Defendant's shotgun because it was making a strange noise. The defendant threw the barrel up to shake it and the gun discharged, hitting his roommate and killing him. Defendant was charged with Manslaughter with a firearm, a second-degree felony, but was only convicted of the lesser included offense of Culpable Negligence, a misdemeanor. The following was argued at sentencing:

Defense Position: This was an accident. Defendant shot and killed his best friend. That is worse punishment than anything that the Court could impose. The Court should have mercy on Defendant, realizing the trauma he's been through and not impose jail time.

State's Position: Someone died here. Defendant is fortunate he is not looking at a prison term; he should at least spend some time in jail. The State is asking for the maximum, 60 days in Leon County Jail.

What do you think? What sentence would you impose, and why? Go ahead and make your notes. I'll wait.

Some of you may have decided, like Judge Hilder, that some jail was appropriate. Reasonable people can disagree. I decided that jail was not necessary or appropriate under the circumstances, either as punishment or as a deterrence. Instead, I placed the defendant on probation and required him to do a substantial amount of community service, which I suggested should include some effort on his part to talk about gun safety.

In another case, the defendant was also charged with Manslaughter with a firearm. Consider the following facts:

The defendant, his best friend, and two other teenagers were riding around in a vehicle at night. The car was driven by the defendant's best friend, S.P. The defendant was in the back seat. He had a pistol in his hand and, depending upon whom you ask, was either trying to un-cock the gun to make it safe, or was playing around with it when it went off. A bullet entered the front driver's seat and the back of defendant's friend, killing him, and causing the car to crash.

The defendant and the other two boys jumped out of the car. They hid the gun and another gun, as well as some cocaine that was in the car. They then fled from the scene. The cocaine was packaged in 24 small bags. One of the firearms, determined to bethe one used to kill the victim, was reported as stolen.

When interviewed later by law enforcement, the defendant denied being in the car. He stated that he had heard that members of a rival gang had chased the victim's vehicle. After being confronted with DNA evidence and other information, the defendant confessed to being inside the victim's vehicle when it crashed. He said another of the boys was playing with the gun and it went off. He also said that the cocaine belonged to this same person.

This account was contradicted by the other boys. It was also contradicted by a recorded phone conversation one of the boys had with the defendant, as well as a phone conversation the defendant had with his mother. The defendant also lied to the victim's parents in the same manner.

The defendant was 17 years old at the time. The defendant had three juvenile cases with charges of battery, disturbing the peace at a school assembly, disorderly conduct and affray. Adjudication was withheld in each case. In his juvenile cases he was given probation and those offenses occurred a few years apart.

At sentencing, the defendant's mother stated: "I understand that my son made a mistake, but he was not the only person in the car. I don't hear them being charged with anything. My son was the only one to come forward and he's the only person being charged. He voluntarily cooperated with the police. He has never been in trouble before. Again, I understand that what he did was wrong. It was an accident, though. I just want to see my baby come home."

Under the sentencing guidelines, Defendant scores a minimum 7 years in prison.

Defense Position: The defendant was 17 when the crime was committed and 19 at the time of sentencing. He has almost no criminal history - only misdemeanors as a juvenile. He is sincerely and extremely remorseful. The victim was his best friend since grade school. He was like a son to the defendant's mother and vice versa for the victim's parents and the defendant. It was an unintentional, accidental shooting. He qualifies for youthful offender sentencing as well as departure because of his age, lack of sophistication in the commission of the crime, and remorsefulness. The defense recommends community control followed by probation, or youthful offender sentencing.

Several members of the defendant's family speak on his behalf, describing him as a warm, loving child growing up, obedient, never in trouble and good student. He has been punished enough just by having the guilt of his friend's death on his hands and putting him in prison would do no one any good.

State's Position: The parents of the victim said that the defendant was like a son, which is why it simply crushed them when he came to their house after the death and denied being in the vehicle and then tried to put the blame on another boy. They, and the State, note also the callousness demonstrated by the defendant who, instead of calling 911 after the shooting and crash, called someone to come pick him up. They also note that the defendant and the other boys had the presence of mind to hide the firearm and the cocaine, but appeared to care little for their dying or dead friend.

The state also suggests that there may be gang affiliation involved here, though they have no substantial proof of that, but they do point out that this was not the all-American good citizen person that the defendant's family points him out to be, as there were four young males driving in a car with cocaine packets to sell and two firearms.

Community control or probation, or even youthful offender is not appropriate under the circumstances. A life has been taken. The defendant should be given a sentence of 20 years.

Well, what sentence would you impose, and why? What facts are mitigating to you and which are aggravating? How do you balance them?

I really don't remember the sentence I imposed, but I can point to the aggravating and mitigating circumstances in my mind. Some are tangible. Some are intangible. The defendant's age is the most obvious mitigator. He was 17 years old at the time of the crime. He had some juvenile history but fairly minor. I'm sure he felt really bad for killing his friend. He didn't do it on purpose.

On the other hand, the circumstances here are much more aggravating than the two preceding cases we looked at. No way to conclude he was engaged in innocent behavior at the time. The gun was stolen. They had cocaine packaged for sale in the car. Worse was his callous behavior after the car crashed, hiding the dope and gun, calling for a ride home but not 911, lying to police and even his friend's parents. His attempt to escape responsibility is not surprising given the mother's defense of him at sentencing. She did her best to minimize his conduct. None of these things bode well for rehabilitation.

The defense suggested a youthful offender sentence would be appropriate. The Youthful Offender statute is aimed at young offenders under the age of 21, placing them in special programs and facilities geared toward rehabilitation, and away from thc more hardened criminals. The maximum sentence you can impose is six years' incarceration. I usually hesitated to go with a YO sentence on the more serious crimes because of the lack of teeth. For example, if I placed a defendant on probation and he violated by something other than a new law violation, I could not exceed the initial prison term. I wouldn't be opposed in this case though because the crime was one of negligence rather than intentional, and because of his age. But even at his young age he deserved some jail time. A lengthy probationary period should follow to make sure he got the message.

Justice and Mercy

When having my portrait painted, I don't want justice, I want mercy.

—Billy Hughes

The Merchant of Venice

Consider this scene from Shakespeare's *The Merchant of Venice.* Shylock has lent money to Antonio, secured by a pound of Antonio's flesh if he defaults—which he does. Shylock has brought the matter to court to collect on his bond. The legal proceedings to enforce the security is before the Duke of Venice, assisted by Portia (disguised as a Doctor of Laws, a judge.)

Portia opines that he is entitled to his bond (the pound of flesh) but urges Shylock to be merciful. When he asks her why he should she gives this famous reply:

PORTIA
The quality of mercy is not strained;
It droppeth as the gentle rain from heaven
Upon the place beneath. It is twice blest;
It blesseth him that gives and him that takes:
'T is mightiest in the mightiest; it becomes
The throned monarch better than his crown:
His sceptre shows the force of temporal power,
The attribute to awe and majesty,
Wherein doth sit the dread and fear of kings;
But mercy is above this sceptred sway;
It is enthronèd in the hearts of kings,
It is an attribute to God himself;
And earthly power doth then show likest God's
When mercy seasons justice. Therefore, Jew,
Though justice be thy plea, consider this,
That, in the course of justice, none of us
Should see salvation: we do pray for mercy;
And that same prayer doth teach us all to render
The deeds of mercy. I have spoke thus much
To mitigate the justice of thy plea;
Which if thou follow, this strict court of Venice
Must needs give sentence 'gainst the merchant there.

Shylock still insists on the security, despite being offered three times the amount of the bond. (He has it in for Antonio for reasons not pertinent for our purposes.) Portia says okay, he can have his justice. He can have his pound of flesh. But just as Shylock is about to put the knife to Antonio, she tells him to wait a bit.

PORTIA
Tarry a little. There is something else.
This bond doth give thee here no jot of blood.
The words expressly are "a pound of flesh."
Take then thy bond, take thou thy pound of flesh,
But in the cutting it, if thou dost shed
One drop of Christian blood, thy lands and goods
Are by the laws of Venice confiscate
Unto the state of Venice.

Oops!

Shylock says, well, in that case, I'll take the offer of thrice the bond. But Portia says no, you wanted justice and justice you shall have.

PORTIA
Therefore prepare thee to cut off the flesh.
Shed thou no blood, nor cut thou less nor more
But just a pound of flesh. If thou tak'st more
Or less than a just pound, be it but so much
As makes it light or heavy in the substance
Or the division of the twentieth part
Of one poor scruple—nay, if the scale do turn
But in the estimation of a hair,
Thou diest, and all thy goods are confiscate.

Shylock says just give him his principal, then, and he'll be on his way. Portia says, nope, you get nothing but the pound of flesh. And she has more bad news for him.

PORTIA
Tarry, Jew.
The law hath yet another hold on you.
It is enacted in the laws of Venice,
If it be proved against an alien
That by direct or indirect attempts
He seek the life of any citizen,
The party 'gainst the which he doth contrive
Shall seize one half his goods; the other half
Comes to the privy coffer of the state,
And the offender's life lies in the mercy
Of the Duke only, 'gainst all other voice.
In which predicament I say thou stand'st,
For it appears by manifest proceeding
That indirectly, and directly too,
Thou hast contrived against the very life
Of the defendant, and thou hast incurred
The danger formerly by me rehearsed.
Down, therefore, and beg mercy of the Duke.

Unlike Shylock, both the duke and Antonio show mercy. The duke spares his life and Antonio waives the forfeiture.

Nobody quite like Shakespeare for delivering a moral so eloquently. And there is certainly poetic justice in this scene, isn't there? Shylock is given every opportunity to be reasonable, to show mercy, and when he doesn't, when he insists on a strict application of the law, on justice, he learns to his regret that the strict application of the law is not always justice.

Some philosophers argue that mercy is a part of justice. Others argue that they are opposing values. I don't know that it matters too much in a practical sense, but I am in the latter camp. Justice is getting what you deserve. Mercy is something you receive when you don't deserve it. If you give a more lenient sentence based on the mitigating circumstances of the crime or the defendant, you are not granting mercy, you are doing justice based on the particular circumstances of the case and of the defendant. The punishment code contemplates taking such circumstances into consideration when arriving at a fair sentence.

Mercy is when you have weighed all the aggravating and mitigating factors, and have arrived at what you think a defendant deserves, e.g., two years in prison, but because the victim asks that you put him on probation, or because you feel sorry for the defendant's pregnant wife and children, who plead for county jail time so he can get work release and support the family, you give a lesser sentence.

Of course, if mercy is not an inherent component of justice, does a judge have the moral authority to grant mercy? Isn't that for the executive branch, as when a governor or a president grants a pardon, or commutes a sentence? What right does the judge have to do anything but justice? Should one's sympathy for a defendant's family be considered in the punishment a defendant should receive?

For those of you who say that mercy is an inherent component of justice, this is not a problem. But even if you say they are opposing values, I think the public expects a sentencing judge to consider what looks like mercy—if it is within reason. And if so, own it. There have been occasions when I have told a defendant point blank that I didn't think he deserved the lesser sentence, but that because of (insert reason) I was going to do so. Perhaps the better way to look at it is that it is not justice versus mercy but punishment or retribution versus mercy. So, two more values to balance in deciding upon a fair sentence.

Corporal Punishment

You may remember several years ago a case in Singapore in which an American was found guilty of a crime and was beat with a cane as punishment. There were cries of protest that it was barbaric and cruel, but others expressed approval and regret that it wasn't used in our country. As an alternative to incarceration, corporal punishment has some advantages.

When you imprison someone as punishment, you punish a number of innocent people. Instead of supporting his family and otherwise contributing to the community, the imprisoned defendant is a drain on our public resources and a negative factor for the economy in general.

So, why can't we impose some sort of corporal punishment? Probably because of the changing norms of what is considered appropriate. It is why it is more and more a rarity in schools, and in homes. It also raises the specter of slavery and the whipping of slaves. It is unlikely we will see this form of punishment play any role in formal sentencing.

The Death Penalty

This is, of course, the ultimate corporal punishment, a subject that has generated much passionate debate, as many people have strong feelings about it one way or the other. I suspect most of you long ago made up your mind, and I will not try to change it here. I only offer my thoughts.

In my opinion, there is a philosophical and practical side to consider. Philosophically, the death penalty is the ultimate example of the eye-for-an-eye theory of retributive justice. If the punishment should fit the crime, there is no substitute for death of the offender if the crime is murder. For the family of the victim, life imprisonment is not enough—well, for some families anyway. They point out that the defendant will still be able to experience many things that their loved one will never be able to experience. That is not justice, they may say. And there is weight to that argument. Before there were official avenues for justice, it took the form of personal revenge, and the urge remains strong.

The flip side of the argument hearkens back to Plato's observation that it is never just to do harm to another, for any reason. Do we teach that killing people is wrong by killing people? To opponents of the death penalty, it is just morally wrong. We should be better than that as a people.

On the pragmatic or practical side, opponents argue that the death penalty is not really a deterrent. I don't buy this argument because it means that one of the key goals of punishment cannot be realized. And because it's impossible to prove a negative. I have to think that, logically, there are those who are deterred from criminal activity because they are afraid of the consequences if they are caught.

My theory is that, as to any particular law, people will generally fall into one of three categories: those who would not break the law because it is morally wrong, regardless of whatever penalty may attach; those who will violate the law if they see an advantage, regardless of the penalty attached; and those who might consider violating the law, but will weigh the benefit against the possible negative consequences.

Let's take speeding. Okay, everyone who has ever exceeded the speed limit, raise your hand. Most of you, if you followed this instruction, would raise your hand, me included. Why do you do that? It is against the law, isn't it? I suspect most of you calculate the negative consequences if you are caught—a fine and points on your driver's license—against the perceived benefit of driving faster. You take a chance, perhaps watching out for troopers or being aware of likely speed traps, but whatever you factor in, you are mindful that the most that will happen is you will have to pay money.

So, what if I told you the Legislature, determining that speed on our highways is a serious threat to public safety, has decided to get tough on speeders. The law now makes speeding a third-degree felony with a mandatory two-year sentence in prison upon conviction.

How many of you will continue to speed? I don't know about you, but I'd be doing a quick cost-benefit analysis and would be very careful not to speed. Speeding is not more morally wrong than it was before, but the sharp increase in the penalty has had the desired deterrent effect.

Consistent with our speeding experiment, I have to think that there are people out there who will do a similar analysis, even if subconsciously, as to other crimes. They might sell drugs, but they wouldn't burglarize a house, for example. Others might commit a burglary, but not a robbery. Some might rob someone but would not murder them. So, there will be one group whose members do not need a penalty to deter them from murder, another for whom the possibility of penalty does not enter into the equation, but yet another group who will be deterred from such an act because they don't want to suffer the punishment if they are caught.

So, in my opinion, the death penalty does offer a deterrent. And philosophically, I have no problem with the argument that a person who murders another deserves to die as his punishment, though I also understand and appreciate the argument that we should be better than that as a society.

The problem to me is more pragmatic. We spend an inordinate amount of time and money on death penalty cases. Because it is the ultimate penalty, the law provides for numerous and varied reviews, which take many years, sometimes decades to complete. And, given that it is the ultimate penalty, there is no do-over if we later discover we made a mistake—which seems to happen with some regularity.

It's not completely satisfactory, but given these considerations, I think we'd be better off making the punishment life in prison with no chance of parole, especially given the significant opposition to it. You'd give up the stronger deterrent, and a bargaining chip for the prosecutor, but you could re-direct a significant amount of time, energy and money to other problems, and you would never put to death an innocent person.

As to other crimes, given the negative consequences to the defendant, his family, and the community that results from incarceration, are there alternatives to, or ways to minimize those negative consequences? Well, yes, if you decide it's appropriate in a given case.

For example, a defendant can be sentenced to a number of days in the county jail, to be served on the weekends. This allows him to continue working and supporting his family. Similarly, for longer periods, work-release programs allow defendants to spend their nights and weekends in jail but allow them to continue in their jobs during the week. These types of programs are sometimes logistically difficult to administer, but it perhaps is worth it. Of course, if a defendant does not have a job, there is no reason not to impose straight time. Probation or community control, a more restrictive form of probation, are alternatives to incarceration, again if you think it's a fair punishment.

Factors to Consider in Sentencing

The Sentencing Guidelines Scoresheet

There are certain facts or information widely thought to be important factors that should be considered in fixing a just sentence. Indeed, many of these are expressly weighed in arriving at the minimum sentence under Florida's Sentencing Guidelines. In every case, a scoresheet is prepared and points assigned based on several factors. These include: the nature of the offense(s) (the more serious, the more points); prior criminal history (the more serious and more numerous, the more points); victim injury, if any (the more serious, the more points); legal status of defendant (not a reference to immigration but rather, if the defendant was on court supervision. e.g., probation, additional points are added). The resultant score determines the minimum sentence.

Downward Departure

Legal reasons for a downward departure from that minimum sentence include: the defendant's minor participation in the offense, a substantially impaired capacity to understand or conform to the law, a need for specialized treatment for a mental or physical condition, substantial cooperation with law enforcement, or the victim's role as the aggressor or provocateur.

So, a judge still has a good bit of discretion within the confines of the sentencing guidelines and there are several intangible factors that might make a difference. Let's explore some of these.

Conduct During Offense

There may be certain offenses that a judge considers serious that don't receive a very high score under the guidelines? For example, I was always amazed at how many prior thefts it took for a thief to score prison time. In many ways, I think those who commit property crimes are more likely to re-offend than those who commit crimes against persons. The former tend to be the result of habitual, lifestyle choices whereas the latter are often the result of spur of the moment bad choices that are less likely to happen again. The law would allow you to impose a harsher sentence for a defendant convicted of theft if that was your view, without having to justify it. Moreover, as noted above, not every burglary, or grand theft, or aggravated battery is the same. Stealing from a church collection plate may seem worse than shoplifting from a department store, yet both might score the same as the level of offense is the same.

The conduct of a defendant during or right after an offense can sometimes tell you a lot about his character and can be an intangible aggravator. I had a case one time of DUI manslaughter involving three marines who had driven over from their base in Georgia for a night of drinking. All three drank too much so it was a toss-up as to who should drive back.

The defendant maintained that he was too drunk to remember who was driving. The jury found, however, that the defendant was the one behind the wheel when it crashed into a tree on I-10. His friend in the front passenger seat was thrown from the car headfirst into the tree and died on the scene. The other passenger was passed out in the back seat.

The evidence at trial included forensics evidence that the defendant, the shorter of the three, was driving at the time of the crash. A motorist who arrived on the scene shortly after the crash testified that as he approached, he saw the defendant exit the vehicle from the driver's side of the car. As the driver came closer, he heard the friend ask the defendant what had happened. The defendant replied that they had had an accident, and that their other friend was dead. The friend, obviously distraught, said, "Oh no, no, no." Then he asked the defendant, "Who was driving?" Without missing a beat, the defendant said, "You were."

The witness said that when he heard that statement the hair on the back of his neck stood up. It chilled me, too, when I heard it in court. And, if the defendant didn't know who was driving, as he claimed at trial, why would he tell his friend that he was the driver? This was not something scored on the sentencing scoresheet, but it was certainly an aggravating factor for me.

Uncharged and Unproved Offenses

There may be evidence at trial that convinces you that the defendant committed one or more additional crimes for which he was not charged. That includes what you think is perjury when the defendant takes the stand at trial and, in your opinion, lies about what happened. What if the jury found him guilty of a lesser crime, but you think he was guilty as charged and don't understand how the jurors came to their decision.

Although it is tempting, you should not punish the defendant for what you thought the evidence showed, but rather what the jury found. To do otherwise is to disrespect the jury and deny the defendant due process. In my experience, there have been times when I was surprised by a jury verdict, but rarely. Mostly, I agreed with them. Jurors, I believe, take their job very seriously, and even if I didn't completely agree with a verdict, I could usually understand why, and I never expressed any disagreement or disappointment in a verdict.

Neither judge nor jury will get it right every time, but we must respect the process. Indeed, that is why our appellate case law forbids a judge from considering criminal conduct that was not charged or charged but for which there was no conviction. Similarly, you should not consider pending charges against a defendant.

I had a case once in which a defendant was charged with several home invasion armed robberies, at least a half dozen. In each, occupants were tied up and had guns pointed at their head while one or more accomplices ransacked the residence. Now, I don't know about you, but to me, this is one of the most serious and aggravating crimes one can commit. You put a gun to someone's head, and they don't know if they are about to die or not. It terrorizes them, humiliates them, robbing them not only of their property but their dignity. I take it very seriously.

When the defendant was convicted, the prosecutor wanted me to sentence the defendant to life in prison—which would have been allowed under the code since armed robbery is a felony punishable by life. The minimum sentence according to the sentencing guidelines score sheet, however, was somewhere around ten years, mainly because the defendant had no prior offenses. He was also young, in his mis-20s as I recall. The prosecutor suggested I should consider the fact that the defendant was charged with several more of these same offenses, and all with aggravating facts, and it showed a very violent tendency and pattern of terrorism. I thought so too but pointed out that the defendant had not been convicted of those other offenses, and that I could not consider them in this sentence. I sentenced him to 10 years in prison.

The State offered him a plea deal on the other robberies, but he rejected it. When he was convicted on a second home invasion armed robbery, I sentenced the defendant to life in prison. One armed robbery is one too many, but two? I believe the defendant was lulled by the first sentence into thinking he would get something similar if convicted a second time. Either his lawyer gave him bad advice, or he wasn't listening—most likely the latter—as anyone who practiced before me understood my position on people who commit armed robberies.

Of course, if the defendant had been found not guilty of the other robberies, he would have received only the ten-year sentence, and that is as it should be. But the evidence was as strong on the others as it was on the first. So, after the second conviction, the defendant resolved the other cases by a plea deal.

As a practical matter, as noted above, a judge can go above the minimum sentence as scored, all the way to the statutory maximum, without having to say why. He or she could give a harsher sentence based on factors that are forbidden by the punishment code, but just not acknowledge it on the record. That would, however, be intellectually dishonest. It would do nothing to help correct what might be seen as an injustice in the current law, because it is done secretly. If you think it should be considered, say so, and why, but follow the law with the hope the law will be changed. Or violate the law and accept the consequences—reversal on appeal and perhaps some disciplinary action by the Supreme Court.

Accepting Responsibility/Remorse

This is probably a big one in most people's minds. It suggests a mindset of a person who is on the road to rehabilitation and thus less likely to re-offend. There are some nuances, however, in this general category worth thinking about. In my opinion, a defendant who confesses early and expresses remorse is less culpable and more deserving of favorable consideration than the defendant who confesses on the eve of trial. And expressing remorse only after being found guilty at trial is not very convincing at all.

A defendant should not, however, be punished for exercising his due process rights, which includes going to trial and requiring the state to meet its burden of proof. If a defendant maintains his innocence, you would, in effect, be punishing him for exercising his due process rights if you faulted him for not taking responsibility or showing remorse for his conduct.

So, accepting responsibility and showing remorse can only be positive factors if demonstrated. The lack thereof should not be considered negative for a defendant who went to trial and was found guilty. At sentencing, you can't expect a defendant who may seek a new trial on appeal to make admissions at sentencing that could be used against him at a new trial. Besides, who would believe him? It's like saying I didn't steal your car, but if I did, I'm sorry.

It is possible, however, to express sympathy for a victim without admitting wrongdoing. It is possible to accept responsibility for your bad conduct without acknowledging it was criminal. It is also possible to maintain your innocence but respect the jury's decision. That might be expecting too much, but I don't think so. The disadvantage of going to trial is that the judge gets to see the evidence and listen to the testimony of the witnesses, including the victim. A trial paints a picture and presents a narrative richer than what appears on the face of a cold record, e.g., a probable cause affidavit or police report. It can make the defendant look worse.

I presided over an attempted murder case in which the defendant was charged with stabbing his estranged girlfriend multiple times in her dorm room. The defendant maintained that he acted in self-defense, but it really was not a very credible defense as the victim was stabbed several times in the back. His explanation was that the back wounds occurred when his girlfriend fell to the floor, on top of the knife. That didn't make any sense to me, and the jury apparently didn't buy it either. They were no doubt more convinced by the testimony of the girlfriend which seemed more logical and was corroborated by the testimony of her roommate who came in in the middle of the attack. The victim was fortunate to have survived.

The defendant's presentation at sentencing was not very appealing, either. As I noted, you can't expect a defendant who maintains his innocence to accept responsibility and show remorse at sentencing, especially when he plans to appeal. But there was absolutely no recognition that the victim had suffered almost two dozen knife wounds and that she could have died, and no expression of sympathy for her at all. It was all about him, about how this "incident" had ruined his life, and what an all-around great guy he was.

The victim, on the other hand, was quite compelling at sentencing, dignified, not vengeful, but wanting justice. I tried to give it to her, with a lengthy prison sentence, followed by probation.

Offender's Character, Background and Circumstances

Do you want to know about a defendant's family and social background, and his character? Certainly, when it's good, the defendant wants you to know about it. When not so good, the prosecutor wants you to know about it. Should there be a discount, so to speak, for defendants who have a lousy childhood or other similar circumstances that were beyond their control? By the same token, is a defendant who comes from a good family and had all the advantages, more culpable?

How should we weigh, if at all, actions taken after the crime? After arrest? After plea? If a defendant, for example, enters a program to treat addiction after his arrest on drug charges, should you consider this at sentencing? Is it a sign that he is accepting responsibility for his conduct and is seeking to address his problem, or is he trying to manipulate things to get a more lenient sentence? Does it matter? Same question for other actions, such as paying restitution to the victim, or registering for school or other educational program.

Whenever a defendant took a hat-in-hand approach at sentencing, said all the right things about accepting responsibility and being remorseful, it was a plus for me. I used to think, and sometimes say, that I didn't know if he was sincere or not, but at least he was smart enough to know what to say. Or more likely, smart enough to follow his lawyer's advice. You'd be surprised how many don't. Certainly, a proactive approach before sentencing, doing the things that are likely to be ordered, cannot hurt, and often will help. Of course, the judge still needs to impose a sentence commiserate to the crime, one that takes it seriously, but this sort of stuff is a positive factor at sentencing for most judges I would think.

A person who commits several crimes in one episode is likely to receive a less harsh sentence than if he committed the same crimes on separate dates. For example, a defendant who is in a barroom fight and injures six people seriously will get a more severe sentence than if he injured only one person, but probably not six times more severe. Why is that? The theory is that, although there may be several crimes, it was just one episode, and often the crimes are interrelated. It is not as bad as if the defendant committed one crime and then sometime later committed another, and later, another. Each time, he had time to think about what he had done, to reflect on it, and decide to change his criminal ways or to continue them.

What about a defendant who is on probation and commits a new offense? Do you aggravate the sentence or give what you would have done if the defendant had stood up at sentencing for the first crime and said, "Don't give me probation, Judge, cause I will not be able to do it." Just give me whatever fair punishment you think I should have." Not many defendants would say that, though I had a few.

Still, should you give him a more severe sentence because he was on probation at the time, or should it be the same as if he committed the first crime, got jail time, got released, then committed the new crime? Since the new crime is a basis for violation of the probation on the first crime, you will end up sentencing for both if the defendant pleads or is found guilty of the new crime. If so, should the new crime result in a consecutive, rather than a concurrent sentence? That is, should the sentence on the new crime begin to run after the sentence for the violation of probation, or should the sentences run at the same time?

If you had given the defendant a short jail sentence instead of probation, there would be no question that the sentence imposed on the second offense would be consecutive, right? If you sentence concurrently, i.e., have the sentences run at the same time, isn't that a variation of, or a form of, the volume discount discussed above? Is that fair? Is it justice? I suggest that it's not like the example above of the bar fight in which the defendant injures six people. There, it was one incident. Here, with a defendant committing a crime while on probation, we have two incidents.

As to sentencing on the original crime, the one for which defendant was placed on probation, my view was that you shouldn't aggravate the sentence beyond what you would have done if the defendant had asked you to give him jail instead of probation at the time of the original sentencing. It may be frustrating to have a defendant to whom you gave a "chance" and put him on probation, violate your trust and commit another crime while on probation, but I think it makes it cleaner to do it this way. By the same token, to be consistent, the sentence for the new crime should generally be consecutive to whatever sentence you give him for the first crime. In other words, he should not benefit from the fact that he was put on probation for the first crime. Now as part of a plea agreement, a defendant may receive a concurrent sentence, but absent the plea agreement, I think consecutive sentences should be the rule rather than the exception.

Juvenile or Adult?

What about age? Studies show that a teenager's brain is just not developed in the part that guards against impulsive behavior. They just don't have the same ability to control themselves. This might make them less culpable, but not any less dangerous. Indeed, a fifteen-year-old with a gun is scarier than a thirty-year-old with one.

So, on the one hand, you want to understand and appreciate the mitigation of youth, but you also have to fashion a sentence that will protect the public. In addition, when we are dealing with a very serious crime, e.g., armed robbery with a firearm, we must take it seriously. We don't want to impose a sentence that suggests we don't.

Consider this hypothetical based on a real case:

An informant's tip led to the arrest in 2022 of Thomas Atkinson for a robbery in which a woman was killed in 1992, a case that had long since gone "cold." At the time of the robbery-murder Atkinson was 13 years old. When he was arrested in 2022 Atkinson was 43 years old, married, by all accounts, a good spouse and father to his son, a good provider, and otherwise a model citizen. He also expresses deep remorse for the killing.

The fundamental question is whether Atkinson should be punished as if he were 13 years old, as he was at the time of the crime, or as a 43-year-old, as he is now. A juvenile offender can be charged as an adult in certain serious cases, and although he was only 13 years old, murder is about as serious as it gets. Still, you would probably consider his young age and lack of maturity a mitigating factor. Would it be fair to also consider the positive or mitigating things he has done in the intervening years?

It does not appear that rehabilitation (he is a valued member of society) or incapacitation (he is not a threat) would be a penal justification if you sentence him as the adult he has become. Kant would say, as we respect him as an individual, he should receive a sentence in balance with his crime, murder. The harm (woman's death) is the same, regardless of the defendant's age. You may also be concerned with general deterrence. What message are you sending if you give a relatively light sentence?

Should Atkinson be rewarded for evading responsibility for his crime for many years? Years that allowed him to establish and enjoy a new life, to build a positive resume as it were? If he had been caught early on, there would be no argument about him being a good husband and father, a model citizen.

What sentence do you think would be fair, and why? There are no right or wrong answers here. We're just seeing what's important to you in arriving at a fair sentence. Go ahead and think about it, then jot it down on a piece of paper. I'll wait.

Okay, you're back.

So, should he be sentenced as if he were a 13-year-old, disregarding the positive things he has done in the intervening years? Or as an adult who committed a terrible crime when he was very young but has shown substantial rehabilitation?

For what it's worth I lean toward the former. I answer the question posed above by saying no, a person who commits a crime should not be rewarded for evading capture for many years.

His age, however, is a mitigator. If charged as a juvenile, you'd be very limited in the sentence. The most he could receive is six years' incarceration. Even if charged as an adult, one so young lacks the maturity to appreciate the consequences of his conduct, or the ability to control his impulses. He is not as culpable as a mature adult, or even an older teenager.

Still, he's old enough to know right from wrong. He may not understand the full consequences of doing it but he knows killing another person is wrong. Murder is our most serious crime and deserves a serious sentence in order to balance the scales and for purposes of general deterrence.

But I can also see and appreciate the other view. If he had not evaded capture, if he had been sentenced when he was 13 or 14 years old, you might have considered the mitigation of youth and given a light sentence, hoping that it would be enough to get him back on track. Here, we have the benefit of hindsight that in some way justifies that optimism. Would he have turned out a model citizen thirty years later if he had received a lengthy prison sentence? But either way, you are still assuming he is a juvenile at the time of sentencing.

In a similar case with a defendant who was 16 years old, with cognitive difficulties, convicted of murder, I imposed a lengthy term in prison, followed by probation for life. There is a big difference between a 13-year-old and a 16-year-old, but not enough to justify a much more lenient sentence.

The difference here is that there is not the same risk of re-offending, the same danger to the public, to require "incapacitation" of the defendant. He has gone 30 years without re-offending. Does this consideration bring us to direct conflict with the principle noted above, i.e., that he shouldn't be rewarded for evading justice, and should be sentenced as if he had been captured right away? Yes, but it is difficult to ignore this reality in coming up with an appropriate sentence. Ideology or general principles must give way to pragmatism sometimes. And this, to my mind, is one of them. I'd be hoping that the victim's family requests leniency, but even without it, the young age at the time of the offense would justify a relatively minimum time of incarceration, followed by a lengthy probation period.

Role of the Victim

In the film, *The Accused,* a woman, played by Jodi Foster, is gang raped at a bar. The prosecutor on the case negotiates a deal in which each defendant pleads to Reckless Endangerment, with a prison sentence of two to five years. The victim hears about it on the news and is livid. She storms over to the prosecutor's home and interrupts a dinner party to confront her about the deal. "What the fuck is reckless endangerment?" The prosecutor responds and says, "It's a felony that carries the same penalty as rape. You wanted me to put them away and that's what I did." She says she did the best she could.

The victim is not buying it. "You don't understand how I feel," she says. "I'm out there with my crotch hanging out and three guys are sticking it to me, and others are laughing and shouting, and you're telling me that's the best you can do. Well, if that's the best you can do, then your best sucks. Now, I don't know what you got for selling me out but I sure as shit hope it was worth it."

It is a compelling scene and watching it you can understand why Jodi Foster won a best actress Oscar for her performance, but this would not happen in the real world. The prosecutor would have gone to her before she even negotiated a deal and discussed the parameters, got her victim to buy in on her strategy. And certainly, she would have consulted with her before making a final deal. That doesn't mean the victim would get a veto. The prosecutor makes the call, but she deserves to at least have a voice.

Should a defendant get a harsher sentence because the victim or the victim's family is more organized and articulate, more respected in the community, or more photogenic? Should it really be a factor in the defendant's sentence whether the victim was a good person and whether so many people loved him or her?

How do we distinguish between emotional versus fact information about the victim? Should we? Does it matter if the victim lost all they had? For example, the theft of $200 from a poor person may be considered worse than $2000 from a rich person. What about the role of the victim in the incident as a mitigating factor? Consider the following hypothetical:

Good friends, Frank and Tom, are playing pool in a bar. Tom is 6' 3" and weighs 250. Frank is much smaller, at 5' 7" and 140. Frank has had a little too much to drink and starts ragging on Tom, accusing him of owing him money, which Tom disputes. Frank calls Tom names. Tom tries to brush it off, but Frank gets more and more belligerent. Finally, Tom says he's had enough and starts to leave. Frank grabs him by the shirt and says, "You're not going anywhere. I'm not done talking to you." Tom punches him in the face and breaks his nose, then leaves. Frank calls the police, files a complaint and Tom is later charged with battery.

There is no question that the elements of battery, striking a person against his will, can be proven. But, admit it, you are a little bit sympathetic to Tom, who endured Frank's needling and his aggressive step in grabbing his shirt to keep him from leaving, right? Probably not enough for Tom to claim self-defense, given their relative size. Hard to think he really felt threatened by Frank, just really annoyed.

But isn't there a little bit in you that thinks old Frank had it coming. I mean if you were Frank's size, would you be putting your hands on someone Tom's size, telling him he's not allowed to leave cause you're not through talking to him? Do you find Tom's conduct less culpable because of the conduct of the victim?

Now, let's change the gender and make Frank, Frances. Are you as sympathetic to Tom as you were when the victim was a man? I suspect not. I'm willing to bet that we would see harsher sentences for the defendant who punched the woman. Not from all of you, but probably most. What does that tell us? Does it indicate a bias? If so, is that a bad thing?

One of the last criminal cases I presided over was in Franklin County. The defendant was charged with attempted murder and aggravated battery. The evidence was conflicting as to what exactly happened, and importantly, who instigated the confrontation between defendant and the victims. The following are some of the relatively uncontested facts:

The victims were part of a group from Wakulla County who had travelled over to Carrabelle, a fishing village in Franklin County, to party. By all accounts, they drank heavily at a local bar and were obnoxious in their behavior. Later, they gathered around a boat docked nearby. At some point, the defendant and his ex-wife came walking by. The victims began to taunt the two. The defendant responded in kind. The versions differ here as to whether one of the victims or the defendant approached the other, but it seems more likely that the one victim started towards the defendant, and the defendant met him half-way.

It seemed that the victim had brought his fists to a knife fight, according to a second victim who was watching from a distance. He ran over when he saw the defendant straddling his friend and about to stab him in the chest. The defendant instead stabbed this second victim when he approached, which had the effect of breaking up the fight. The defendant then fled the scene.

Pointing out the fact that he was rather diminutive in size compared to the two victims, and suffered from debilitating arthritis, the defendant claimed he acted in self-defense. I denied his motion under the stand your ground statute to bar prosecution, and the jury rejected this defense, finding him guilty of a lesser included charge of attempted manslaughter. Even with the lesser charge, he scored a significant number of years in prison according to the sentencing guidelines, based in part on the fact that he had a previous conviction for which he had served some twenty years in prison.

The defendant argued at sentencing for a downward departure based on the statutory ground of victim contribution to the crime. I listened to the arguments, to the mother of one of the victims, who acknowledged that her son had a drinking problem which sometimes led to trouble. I heard from numerous friends and family members in the Carrabelle community who spoke of the many good works and deeds the defendant had performed in the past, good Samaritan type stuff that belied the violent criminal his record might suggest. That was a long time ago, they assured me, and he was a changed man.

I was impressed with the broad support for the defendant in his community. I had also been impressed with the defendant's demeanor throughout the various court proceedings. And I agreed with the defense that the victims' conduct, while not sufficient to justify the claim of self-defense, did contribute substantially to the event. Specifically, had they not been very drunk and so antagonistic and willing to have an altercation, there would not have been one and they would not have been injured. I concluded that a downward departure was appropriate, that the defendant and the community would be better served by a long term of probation more than a long prison term. I figured if I had misread the defendant and the circumstances, he would violate his probation quickly and be back before me. For a lot of reasons, I hoped he didn't. And I ran into his attorney recently and was pleased to hear that his client was still doing good deeds in the community and staying out of trouble.

Over the years, there has been quite a push to give alleged victims certain rights by law, including the right to be informed of the proceedings, to be consulted as to any plea offers, and to be entitled to speak at sentencing. These are all things which I think, as a matter of courtesy, should be done anyway, and I don't think a law should be needed. But apparently others thought otherwise and passed laws to this effect. And now, in

Florida and other states, we have a constitutional provision protecting "victim rights" which is called Marsey's Law.

I was not in favor of this amendment. The language in it was, in my opinion, exceedingly vague, with many, many questions about what it really means. Subsequent litigation has proved me correct. We now have competing constitutional provisions regarding accused persons and those we call victims—which is another problem as they are really alleged victims unless and until an accused admits to the crime or is convicted of it. How are these conflicting provisions to be reconciled?

This constitutional amendment, as with a good number of laws, bears the name of a victim whose family made it a mission to get a law passed in honor of their family member. Although I am sympathetic to these people, I don't think many of these laws are needed. Rather, good faith, common sense enforcement of current laws would suffice. Certainly, no constitutional provision was necessary in Florida, where we already had strong laws giving alleged victims certain "rights' to participate in proceedings.

But "victim rights" sounds very appealing. I mean, who could be against it? So, it passed, and the result will be more confusion, more complexity, more inefficiencies, more disputes, and more litigation, which will take more time and money to resolve.

Cash Register Justice

Is it appropriate to consider cost? Shouldn't we be good stewards of public monies? If so, how much weight do we give it? Are efficiency and cost-effectiveness legitimate factors to consider in sentencing? If effectiveness is important, how do we predict and measure it?

If a defendant has severe medical problems, does that affect whether he gets County Jail, Department of Corrections time, or probation? Many times, prosecutors will recommend to the judge at sentencing that the defendant receive one year and one day, which means prison, as opposed to eleven months and twenty-nine days in the county jail. This is especially true if the defendant has medical issues requiring expensive treatment. The reason is money. The sheriffs, especially those in small counties, do not have the resources to take care of the prisoner in the county jail. If they are sentenced to prison, it becomes the responsibility of the Department of Corrections.

Similarly, those normally law and order types who want to put everybody in jail and advocate high bail amounts sing a different tune when a defendant awaiting disposition of his case has serious medical problems that will tax the budget. Then the law and order crowd is okay with an ROR (release on own recognizance in order to avoid having to pay the inmate's medical bills. Of course, the defendant rarely has the financial ability to pay either, so some government agency will have to pay. It is just shifting it somewhere else. And it's not as if the danger to the community and/or flight risk which prompted the setting of the bail amount, is now less. It is strictly a cost saving measure on the part of the local sheriff.

It is a reality, and if the prosecutor requested that a defendant be released ROR, I would generally go along with it, though I may request that he or she state the reason on the record. I also am sympathetic to the financial realities faced by a sheriff in a small county. This doesn't make it fair, or just, or good public policy. Likewise, as to the 11/29 in county jail versus a year and a day in prison. It seems to me the tail wagging the dog to base a sentence, or pre-trial release conditions, on such financial considerations.

I've always thought that, all things being equal, it is better to keep a defendant in county jail, close to home, where his family can visit him, rather than send him to the Department of Corrections. We shouldn't allow the inefficiencies of our bureaucracy to dictate our punishments, to, in effect, make that punishment less effective. If it was up to me, almost all correctional facilities would be local, and with much smaller populations. In addition to making it easier to maintain family ties, it makes work release, restorative justice, and other rehabilitative programs easier to implement.

I don't think that large, secure structures are the most cost-efficient way to go, nor the most effective for any of the explicit purposes of sentences, either. These large institutions, with their large populations, are difficult to manage. They tend to dehumanize and fulfill the old cliché that you are reduced to a number. Interactions between those incarcerated and those who guard and supervise them tend to be superficial at best. Everything is geared toward maintaining order and routine, and uniformity. There is little time, resources, or inclination to do much more. It is a bureaucracy within a bureaucracy, with all its mind-numbing rules that often make little sense in individual cases.

And let's face it, a lot of these people are in prison because they have difficulty following the rules. Some are clever and enterprising and always searching for ways around, for angles, for leverage to improve their situation. In such an environment, and with the ratio of inmates to guards, is it any wonder that contraband is smuggled in, employees are corrupted, and gangs form to enforce informal rules within the institution? Is it any wonder that a large percentage of inmates will reoffend within a short period of time after their release? Isn't it obvious that this is not a good model for success in terms of rehabilitation?

Of course, some will say, we don't care about rehabilitation, we care only about punishment. In response I would only point out that eventually the vast majority of those people will be released. Don't you think that it is better for all of us if we can improve the chances that they will not return to crime? And it's not like smaller facilities will cost more. They should cost less. Moreover, a lot of prisoners do not need to be housed in a super-secure facility. They are not a danger to the community. If they escape, they are likely to be captured again. They know that, and they know they will be charged with a new crime and will be in longer and lose a lot of the benefits they have.

I can just hear some of you laughing now, making fun of this Pollyanna view of these people. You say a slap on the wrist is the wrong message to send, that we can't afford to be soft on crime, or criminals. That is not the message. I am a firm believer in actions having consequences. So, this suggestion about where and how we incarcerate people is not from some bleeding heart that thinks everyone is an angel and all we need is love to make things right. It is not being soft on crime, just smarter. Logic tells you, or tells me anyway, that a smaller facility, with a larger employee to inmate ratio, is going to be easier to manage and more likely to serve the purposes of both punishment and rehabilitation.

If something's not working very well, we should be looking for ways to improve it, and our current mass incarceration in large institutions does not seem to be working that well. The rate of recidivism (reoffending) is quite high. We should not be afraid to experiment, to seek out new ways to achieve our shared goals of justice.

Another area in which money seems to be running the show, to the detriment of justice, is what I call policing and prosecuting for profit. It stems from the general idea popular with those in the legislature and the general populace as well, that people who commit crimes should have to pay the cost we have to bear in arresting, prosecuting, and housing them. That seems fair on its face, and I have no problem with the concept, but in practice, I believe it has unintended, negative consequences on our shared notion of justice.

It is the basis for many forfeiture laws, which allow law enforcement to seize property used to facilitate a crime—cars, boats, cash, etc. This happens a lot in drug cases, where a defendant drives his car to make a sale, or uses his boat to transport the drugs, or stores them in his house. The only limit is the creativity of the law enforcement agency involved. And the burden of proof in a forfeiture proceeding is a preponderance of the evidence, a lower burden of proof than beyond a reasonable doubt, which is required for conviction of the crime itself.

The problem is that law enforcement agencies depend on these forfeitures to help fund their agencies. So, there is an incentive to go after these cases because they are profitable for them in a monetary sense. On a smaller scale, many of you have no doubt experienced a "speed trap" in which you were ticketed for speeding and convinced that the motivation was not safety on the highways but rather money for the local government.

It's just so much worse if the government takes something of more value. And often, when government agents take a car, for example, they are not only depriving a defendant of his only transportation, they are depriving his family as well. Too bad, you say, that's what happens when you break the law. And it is true that there are many collateral consequences of criminal conduct far beyond whatever sentence is imposed on the defendant, especially if it involves incarceration for any length of time. The family also must suffer. Is that fair? Maybe not, we say, but it is the fault of the defendant, not those of us who demand that the wrongdoer be appropriately punished.

We also demand that a defendant pay the cost of prosecution and the cost of his defense in criminal cases. Now, in the run-of-the-mill case, these are very nominal sums—maybe

$200.00, much less than the actual cost, but there are also fines and court costs that are tacked on by law for every sentence. Now we are talking several hundred dollars in most cases, much more in others. And sometimes a prisoner is charged for the cost of his incarceration. There may also be restitution to the victim, property stolen or damaged, personal injuries, etc. No one can argue with the fairness of this requirement, at least in concept. It fits right in with notions of restorative justice and rehabilitation.

If you are on probation, you must pay the cost of your supervision, which is typically about $50.00 per month. If you are incarcerated, you are expected to defray that cost as well with a nominal fee of $50.00 a day. Your probation terms may require you to complete various programs or counseling or treatment, and you are expected to pay at least something towards those costs as well. If you are prohibited from going around certain people or places, you may be required to pay the cost of electronic monitoring of your location.

Many times, these programs are offered in locations far away from your residence, and the only vehicle you had was seized as part of your case. You must depend on public transportation or family and friends with vehicles, to get you there—and to your monthly appointments to your probation officer. If you happen to have a driving offense, DUI or Driving While License Suspended or Revoked (DWLSR), for example, you can't drive anyway because your license will be suspended for a time as part of your sentence. And if your license was suspended for non-payment of fines, you'll have to pay those up, plus a reinstatement fee.

Bad check cases are another good example. If you write a check when you know you don't have the funds in your account to cover it, the bank charges you a fee, the business charges you a fee, and the prosecution will want its fee for prosecuting the case, and certainly restitution to the person or business will be required. All this for someone who obviously didn't have the money to start with, or they wouldn't have written a bad check.

Again, this is not to say that the concept is not sound in theory and can be helpful in restoring some balance on the justice scale, in forcing a defendant to accept responsibility for his conduct. My point is that it is one thing to punish a person for their wrongful conduct, but quite another to crush them, to make it virtually impossible for them to make it back into the community with the rest of us. Most criminal defendants are poor, and unable to pay more than a token amount toward the cost of the arrest, prosecution, incarceration and supervision. When we saddle these costs on defendants, it is neither just, nor prudent, and in many cases downright cruel.

Well, you might say, aren't most of these sentences the result of a plea agreement? Didn't the defendant agree to this as part of the sentence? He shouldn't have agreed to it if he couldn't do it. But most defendants are looking to get out of jail—where they have been since arrest—-or they want to avoid a jail sentence. They hear "probation" and they are on it like white on rice. This, even though the judge may explain the conditions and inquire about their ability to comply. They literally will agree to anything and say anything sometimes to get it over with.

Indeed, I've had some prosecutors admit that they offer probation in a case that might be a little weak for them, confident that the defendant will later violate probation and can be given a harsher sentence then. The burden of proof in a violation of probation case is a preponderance of the evidence, much lower than having to prove the original crime. That seems just wrong, though the State will argue that if the defendant does what he has agreed to, he gets off easy. Again, we are talking rough justice, very rough justice, compromises that have to do with self-interest more than fairness, with the hope that you achieve something close to real justice.

In the early days of our republic, it wasn't uncommon to jail people who couldn't pay their debts, and a person would often be given a sentence of 30 days or $30.00 in a criminal case. So, the advantage in our society of having wealth, and the disadvantage of the converse is not a new thing. It ripples through every aspect of society, determining where you live, where and how you are educated, the level of health care you receive, and your chances of becoming a victim of crime, to list just a few examples. Why would it be any different in the justice arena.

It's even worse, really, for the middle class, who will not be poor enough to qualify for the public defender but can't really afford an attorney. That in itself will be an extreme economic burden, on top of the amount necessary to bond out of jail. There is no legal insurance, either, like for healthcare, and even if there was, most people would not see the advantage of paying an insurance premium each month on the off chance they will need a lawyer later.

If you are rich, you can afford to hire the best attorneys and wage the costly legal battle. If you are sufficiently poor—indigent is the official term for it—you get the services of an attorney for free. And if you are incarcerated, you have a lot of time on your hand and will insist that your attorney file every appeal or motion possibly available to you. After all, you have nothing to lose.

The folks in the middle, though, the ones who don't qualify for a free lawyer, but do not have the money to wage their legal battles, will have to weigh the chance of success at trial or on appeal against the cost. It is contrary to our professed ideals, but the reality should come as no surprise. You try to minimize the adverse effects of poverty as best you can, but as the above illustrates, those without relative financial means are always at a disadvantage in receiving justice.

Recently, the voters in Florida approved a constitutional amendment restoring to convicted felons the right to vote upon completion of their sentence. Because the amendment did not specify what it meant for a person to have completed his sentence, the Legislature decided the amendment was not self-executing and needed "implementing legislation" to clarify what that meant. Predictably, they said it included the payment of all restitution, court costs and fines. I disagree with both the premise that implementing legislation was required, and the interpretation that completion of a sentence means you must have paid all fees, fines and costs imposed as part of that sentence.

Whether a law is passed by the Legislature or by the voters, its interpretation is a function of the judiciary. Lord knows there are laws passed every year by the Legislature whose language is vague and ambiguous, and it is up to a court, in a specific case, to interpret it. It's fundamental to the separation of powers for the three branches of government. So, unclear language in a "law" passed by the voters does not mean the Legislature must clarify it.

On the second point, reasonable people can disagree on the amendment's meaning, specifically, what it means to have completed a sentence. A local federal judge disagreed with the Legislature but the federal appeals court reversed him and upheld the law. For what it's worth, I think the Legislature and the appellate court got it wrong, on two fronts.

As a matter of construction, the ordinary understanding of when a sentence has been completed is when the period of incarceration and/or probation has ended, specifically when the government no longer has the hold of authority over the defendant. The hang-up was the language about completing the *terms of sentence,* which usually includes the fines and court costs or restitution assessed as part of the sentence. If you haven't paid these monies, you haven't completed your sentence. That is how it was interpreted by the Legislature and the appellate court.

This seems reasonable on its face, but it ignores the reality that a probationary term may be completed without all conditions having been met, including payment of monies ordered. You may or may not have paid all monies or successfully met all conditions of your probation, but for a variety of reasons, the term of probation has ended.

Some defendants complete all conditions of their sentence, even getting an early termination of their probation, but many more never do, including failing to pay all their fines and fees. If the failure is willful, they may receive additional jail time. If the failure is not willful, if they were simply unable to do so through no fault of their own, there is no additional sanction because, as noted above, a violation of probation must be intentional. To do otherwise is to create, in effect, a debtors' prison, which our law has long since abolished. In some cases, there is no sanction because the State dropped the ball and was unable to prove their case.

At most, in either case, the amount owed is reduced to a civil judgment and probation is terminated. The court no longer has any authority over the defendant. It is sort of like being discharged from the army. It may be an honorable or a dishonorable discharge, but either way, you are no longer in the army. You have completed the terms of your military service. Similarly, it is cleaner, and more in keeping with what is ordinarily meant to have completed a sentence, to say it means when the court no longer has authority over you.

Another complicating factor pointed out by the trial judge was that the State was unable to tell the convicted felons who brought suit exactly how much they owed. So, you are telling them, you can't vote until you have paid all monies ordered as part of your sentence, but we can't tell you how much that is.

As a matter of policy, of justice, the Legislature's interpretation means that most felons will never get their right to vote back, because they will never be able to pay. I know this stance is consistent with the popular stance that defendants should be made to pay for the cost of their prosecution, but as pointed out before, I think it is unwise. It is cutting off our noses to spite our faces. If one of our goals is to bring our offenders back within the common moral sphere, to give them a stake in society, motivation to be a constructive, participating member, we will have squandered this opportunity by placing obstacles before them that they are unable to overcome. I think that is a mistake in terms of the long-term health of society.

Shooting an Elephant and Playing to the Audience

Based on George Orwell's experience as the sub-divisional police officer with the Indian Imperial Police, *Shooting an Elephant* is set in Moulmein, a town in the British colony of Burma. Because he is a military occupier, he is hated by many in the village, and they regularly hurl insults at him as he walks down the street. He finds this somewhat ironic as he was "all for the Burmese and all against their oppressors, the British." He hates his job.

Orwell's job, in this instance, is to respond to a report of a rogue elephant which has been causing damage in the town. Orwell heads toward the affected area. On the way, locals explain that the elephant is not wild, but rather a domesticated one that has had an attack of "musk." "Musk" occurs when tame elephants, held in chains, break their restraints and go berserk. Its "mahout," or handler, pursued it in the wrong direction and is now twelve hours away. On its rampage, the elephant has destroyed public and private property and killed livestock.

To make matters worse, Orwell learns that the elephant has also killed a "coolie" who Orwell observes in the mud, "lying on his belly with arms crucified and head sharply twisted to the side." Orwell feels the pressure from the crowd urging him to shoot the elephant, but he senses that the elephant is probably no longer dangerous. He concludes that "it would be murder to shoot the elephant." But, despite Orwell's aversion to shooting the elephant, he also understands that he will lose face and be humiliated if he does not shoot it. He will appear weak and less powerful in the eyes of the villagers. He therefore shoots the elephant.

The death is an ugly, protracted fiasco. After three shots, the elephant still does not die. Orwell fires his two remaining shots into the elephant's heart. He sends someone to get his small rifle, then pours "shot after shot into his heart and down his throat." Still, the elephant does not die. Orwell, unable to stand the elephant's suffering and unable to watch and listen to it, goes away.

Orwell's fellow British police officers all believe he did the right thing. Orwell is relieved, he admits, that the coolie died, because it gave him a pretext for shooting the elephant. As far as the villagers are concerned, he saved face. Yet Orwell concludes, "I often wondered whether any of the others grasped that I had done it solely to avoid looking a fool."

Most of the people in the courtroom, or in the general public following a case at sentencing, want the judge to be "tough" in imposing a sentence. The defendant and his friends and family don't, of course, but they are in the minority, for sure. Just as Orwell felt pressure from the villagers, judges feel pressure to give significant jail time in many cases whether the circumstances of the charge and the defendant justify it or not. Many people don't do nuance when it comes to sentencing.

They hear a little something about what the defendant is alleged to have done, and they have a visceral reaction as to how he should be punished.

In many cases that creates no moral conflict for a judge as the judge shares the sentiment. He or she feels a significant prison sentence is appropriate. There will be cases, however, in which a judge sees little value in a lengthy prison sentence. That's when the pressure comes to "hammer" a defendant to satisfy the public lust for retribution. Just like Orwell, the judge does not want to lose face, to appear weak and labeled soft on crime. It is something a judge should, in my opinion, address, internally and externally.

We expect our judges to have moral courage and to exercise independent judgment, without bowing to pressure from any person or group. We expect this even when that group is large and vocal and may hold your professional future in their hands. We expect this even if these people threaten you with violence. Keeping that independent judgment is not so easy at times, but that's when it is most needed.

So, when faced with a public clamor for blood, or any similar situation where a sentence or order is likely to be unpopular, the best a judge can do is explain the decision. If that's not good enough for some people, so be it. You will have done what you thought was right. The best safeguard against this pressure is an informed electorate who realizes that this independent judgment is essential to justice, and they are committed to protect it against attack.

Regardless, there is no question that the sentence imposed sends a message, to the defendant and to the general public. The sentence itself sends a message. But if we are concerned with the perception that justice has been done, shouldn't we explain the aggravating and mitigating factors we have considered and why we arrived at the particular sentence? I think so.

Judges certainly have different, competing constituencies, different audiences with different expectations at a sentencing. The defendant always wants leniency, and the victim almost always wants you to put the defendant under the jail. The defendants and their lawyers want you to take whatever time is necessary to hear what they have to say. The prosecutors, too, for the most part. The clerks and the bailiffs have their view of what the sentence should be, but mostly, they want the judge to move things along and get through the docket. If a bailiff remarks that you are a very patient person, it is not a compliment. It means he thinks you let the lawyers and defendants talk too much.

The lawyers, in general, would like you to see things their way, of course, if they can, but they expect you to at least be consistent and decisive. The general public is probably more in line with the bailiffs and clerks, in terms of not wasting a lot of time with individual defendants, and with the prosecution in wanting stiff sentences, but not all of them. Indeed, I don't mean to paint a broad brush for any of these groups. Most have their preferences, but they also understand the need to balance competing goals or preferences.

If you are an elected judge, you do not want to perceived as soft on crime. It's a good way to draw opposition in your next election. The reality is, there is not a big voting block who want you to be more lenient on criminals—mostly criminals and their families, and their attorneys.

And notice I say *perceived* as being soft on crime. There may be some judges who tend to give more lenient sentences, but none are doing so to be soft on crime. They are just trying to be smarter on crime, more effective, trying to reduce the cost to society of warehousing criminals, and reducing recidivism. Moreover, judges don't like crime or criminals, but they respect the law and have taken an oath to follow it. Many judges are painted as being soft on crime simply for following the law, e.g., suppressing evidence obtained in violation of the constitution.

If you checked with prosecutors and defense attorneys who practiced before me, I don't think they would describe me as lenient in my sentences. But I hope they would say I was fair, and consistent, and that I protected a defendant's due process rights. I certainly tried to. But as noted, there will always be different constituencies, different audiences to a sentence. The perception of whether a sentence was fair will often depend on how it was delivered. This is why I say you should explain how you arrived at the sentence.

The parties, the prosecution and the defense, deserve an explanation so that your decision does not appear arbitrary. Even if they disagree with your decision, they can at least see there was some logic to it. It also serves to guide the lawyers in future cases. Most people would agree that defendants similarly situated should receive similar sentences. And, if the case goes up on appeal, the appellate court will have the benefit of your reasoning.

Aside from confirming that it was not an arbitrary decision, I think there is also real value to expressing the collective moral indignation of the community at the conduct of a defendant where warranted. There is value in seeing our collective moral values re-enforced by someone in authority, like a judge.

There is a feeling among some judges that the less said, the less likely you will say something that the appellate court can take issue with, and the less likely you will be reversed on appeal. This may be true, but I find it a little intellectually dishonest. A judge shouldn't be afraid of being reversed. We do the law and justice no good service by keeping quiet as to our reasons. Besides, I think appellate courts are more likely to give the benefit of the doubt to judges who articulate the reasons for their conclusions on the record, in terms of the exercise of discretion, as opposed to having to guess at how a judge arrived at a conclusion.

There is a right way and a wrong way to send a message with your comments at sentencing and express the moral indignation of the community at the defendant's conduct. Notice I said the conduct, not the defendant himself. It is a subtle distinction, but I think important to make. As tempting as it might be, and satisfying to do so, we should avoid attacking or demeaning the defendant as a person. There are exceptions, of course. Some defendants have shown a pattern of conduct so bad you are convinced that they are evil incarnate, and you say so.

But most defendants are not evil. They are not bad people. Rather, they made bad choices and did bad things. And they should be called on it. But you should concentrate on what they did rather than who they are. To do otherwise is to be disrespectful, and to suggest there is no hope for rehabilitation. That might be a little too nuanced for some people. They might argue that you are what you do. If you do something bad, you are bad. And as I say, there are instances when a repeated pattern of conduct supports a conclusion about a person's basic character.

It certainly is more dramatic and entertaining for those in the audience when a judge lights into a defendant on a personal level. As a lawyer I remember a judge telling one defendant that he was "lower than whale excrement." It was colorful and creative, and it has stuck with me all these years. Similarly, the quote from Judge Roy Bean below has a certain poetry about it and probably expressed the sentiment of his community quite well.

There are many video clips on You Tube of real judges expressing their righteous indignation at defendants before them. In one, the judge saves his harshest words for the mother of a child victim sexually assaulted by her boyfriend.

He gives the boyfriend a life sentence with very little comment, then lays into the mother so hard you'd think she was the defendant. And it's clear the judge believed she should have been.

Not that the mother's actions in allowing in a man into her home who she knew to be a sex offender didn't warrant admonishment. But the judge was so excited and angry I thought his head might explode. Like I say, there is a right and wrong way to go about it. That kind of intemperate behavior by a judge in Florida would probably earn him a public reprimand from the Supreme Court.

Probation Conditions

If you are placed on probation, there are, by law, certain general conditions that will apply in every felony case, including no violation of the law, no intoxicants to excess, no illegal drugs, maintain lawful employment, and report as required to the probation officer. In addition, the judge who places a defendant on probation has a good amount of discretion as to what, if any, special conditions to impose.

Theoretically, they are imposed for the purposes of rehabilitation and protecting against further criminal activity. They vary depending on the nature of the crime and other circumstances specific to the defendant. Some common terms or conditions include community service, restitution, and no contact with the victim, individual or group counseling, curfew, and drug treatment. These special conditions are imposed by the judge in her discretion, but often they are part of the plea agreement.

One of the problems is that when we overload defendants with probation conditions, it increases the chance that they will fail. And what purpose does that serve? Isn't it a little paternalistic, too, and invasive, to decide that a defendant needs certain programs or activities, or curbing of certain habits? Why is it that we don't just impose the punishment—incarceration, or some curtailment of their freedom via house arrest, community control (a more intense form of probation) and let them decide if and how they need to address any perceived problems or obstacles to a future law-abiding life, and how to go about it? It's called personal responsibility.

In many cases, I think some probation conditions are almost rote, the going rate for commission of certain crimes. You shoplift; you take anti-theft class. You hit your wife; you do a batterers' intervention program. You get in some other fight; you do an anger management course. You possess drugs; you do screening and evaluation and treatment if recommended. I don't think that this one size fits all approach is effective, and I think there is a hint of punishment in some of these, disguised as rehabilitation.

That does not mean that there are not some good things to come out of imposing these conditions. While we may want to place the responsibility on the individual defendant to rehabilitate himself, some benefit from the extra push to get the help they know they need but may be too weak to do it on their own. And some of these services are not readily available outside of the criminal justice system. If a drug addict or a person with mental health issues wants to seek treatment, there is almost nothing available to him without great cost, usually beyond his means. But if they commit a crime, we make it available as part of probation.

But don't we have it backwards? If treatment was readily available for those who sought it, at a cost they could afford, we might have fewer crimes related to addiction or mental health problems. And it takes away one more excuse for a defendant who wants to blame drug addiction for his crime. I believe that a person must sincerely want help with a problem before court-mandated help will be successful. Not always, but most of the time.

Do you think defendants lie at sentencing and tell the judge that they want help with their drug or other problem in order to avoid a harsher sentence? Sure, they do. At least some of them. Who wouldn't? I used to test defendants who told me this by saying that I planned to impose some significant period of incarceration, but that if they really wanted drug treatment, I could provide for that in a probationary period to follow. If they were serious, they would say yes. If they weren't, they would say no. They wanted drug treatment instead of jail time, not in addition to jail.

My theory was that you should fix a punishment that was appropriate for the crime, then offer a probationary term in order to assist the defendant in whatever rehabilitation he seeks, whether that be fighting addiction or mental health treatment, or help with vocational or educational efforts. Such an approach harmonizes the desire for both consistency and individualization in sentences. There is societal value in having a set punishment range, regardless of other factors, and then individualizing a sentence relative to probationary terms or other rehabilitation and reform efforts, depending on the situation of each defendant.

What about the conditions of incarceration? There is not a lot of sympathy in the general public for inmates. Prison is a bad place, people will say, which is why you should not commit crimes that will take you there. They complain that prisoners have it too easy. They get free food, health care, exercise, television and other entertainment. They are not required to work like the rest of us for these things, either. Shouldn't there be some deprivation as punishment while incarcerated? Shouldn't a prisoner be required to earn some privileges? Shouldn't he be required to contribute to his keep?

On the other hand, shouldn't they be protected from physical and psychological torture, beatings, and rapes at the hands of fellow inmates? Isn't the deprivation of liberty itself supposed to be the punishment? As one of my former colleagues used to put it, we send people to prison *as* punishment, not *for* punishment. Going only on what is depicted in film and television, the prisons in Britain and Europe come closer to this premise, seem to preserve for them a little more dignity. For example, they seem to allow prisoners to wear their own clothes rather than a uniform jumpsuit, have televisions and other personal items in their cell, and allow them to walk about more freely than in American prisons.

All of these are important considerations if we are interested in reducing recidivism. Unless they are in for life, these prisoners are coming back into society someday. How they are treated during their incarceration will have a significant impact on what type of person we get, how likely he or she is to re-offend, and how quickly.

Restorative Justice

Restorative justice is an approach that focuses on the needs of the victims and the offenders, as well as the involved community, rather than just punishment of the offender. The goal is for them to share their experience of what happened, to discuss who was harmed by the crime and reach a consensus as to what the offender can do to repair the harm. This may include a payment of money given from the offender to the victim, apologies and other amends, and other actions to compensate those affected and to prevent the offender from causing future harm.

A restorative justice program aims to get offenders to take responsibility for their actions, to understand the harm they have caused, to give them an opportunity to redeem themselves and to discourage them from causing further harm. For victims, its goal is to give them an active role in the process and to reduce feelings of anxiety and powerlessness. Restorative justice is founded on an alternative theory to the traditional methods of justice, which often focus on retribution. However, restorative justice programs can complement traditional methods. It is not suitable in every case, and you need buy-in by the victim, the defendant, the prosecutor, and the community.

Is it a naïve perspective on human nature? Is it some touchy-feely thing that is just an excuse for a lesser sentence? Some of you may be skeptical, but studies suggest it makes offenders less likely to reoffend. It also has the highest rate of victim satisfaction and offender accountability of any method of justice. In a sense, it is simply another way to achieve the purpose of rehabilitation. It does not have to substitute for the retributive purpose of punishment, but if it works, why not allow it to complement the retribution and assist in rehabilitation? After all, we want to impose a punishment befitting the crime, but in the end, we want to bring the offender back into the fold, to bring him back inside the moral sphere of mutual respect and adherence to the rules we have agreed upon. Isn't that to everyone's benefit?

Therapeutic Courts

In recent years, we have seen the rise of specialty courts that are geared to a specific group of offenders or category of crime—mental health court, drug court, veterans' court, etc. There was a good bit of resistance to this "therapeutic" approach from prosecutors, and others, who saw this as being soft on crime, and letting criminals off too easy, but there is a deeper, philosophical objection that is worth exploring, specifically, what is the proper function of the courts.

Some would argue that the role of the courts is to adjudicate, period. It is unreasonable, and unrealistic to ask courts to go further. When they do more than enter orders, they enter areas traditionally the province of the executive branch, or sometimes that of the Legislature, and tend to forget their place in the scheme of government and do mischief. You may recall the words of President Andrew Jackson when he was informed that the Supreme Court, headed by Chief Justice John Marshall, had ruled contrary to Jackson's plans to remove the Cherokee Indians from the southeast to the west: "John Marshall has made his decision; now let him enforce it!"

This statement brings into perfect clarity what Alexander Hamilton had observed in *The Federalist Papers* about the judiciary, i.e., that the courts have neither the sword nor the purse, but only judgment. They are dependent upon acceptance of their rulings by the executive branch, so that the orders may be enforced. When the Supreme Court said that separate was no longer equal and ordered the integration of public schools in Little Rock, Arkansas, things might have gone differently if President Eisenhower had not accepted the ruling and committed the authority of the executive branch to its enforcement.

Others say that the courts need to be flexible and change with the times, to collaborate with others to achieve public policy goals. Indeed, people continue to come to court for some form of relief or remedy when the other branches have not provided it. Courts have overseen the busing of children across communities in order to enforce desegregation of schools and re-written re-districting maps for legislative bodies. It is a natural extension of the function of the court in providing a remedy for a wrong.

In civil cases, it leads to expansive injunctive orders with regular review by the court, and in family law cases, especially those involving children, to more detailed and intrusive managing of the lives of its members. In criminal cases, it has led to the court taking a more active role in supervising defendants and intervening in their lives to remedy whatever personal problems they have. It's a noble goal, but the courts cannot be the answer to all of society's ills, nor should they take the place of the executive in this respect.

The debate is academic at this point because the courts are far down that path and the line between judicial and executive function continues to blur. If we are more interested in results than in "staying within lanes" there are some common components or aspects of the therapeutic model that I think work well. First, the emphasis is on correcting behavior, addressing the problem that resulted in the violation of law—other than the rather simplified response that the defendant made a bad choice—so that there is less chance of recidivism.

Second, sanctions for violation of the rules are mild, e.g., a weekend in jail rather than six months, and the person is still in the program, with the understanding that a lot of people will fail. The sanctions are graduated in severity, and eventually, a person may be kicked out of the program, but the assumption is that many people will not make it without a few mistakes or slips. The sanctions are meant to encourage and deter at the same time.

More importantly, the punishment is swift, and certain. The defendants know what to expect because it's in the agreement they signed to be in the program, and most of the time they accept the punishment without complaint because they know they messed up. A less severe, but swift and sure punishment is much more effective in correcting behavior than a harsher punishment that may or may not occur and is a long time in coming. The length of time between crime and the traditional sentence after a trial can be quite lengthy, years in some serious cases, and at least several months.

The other key component is that the defendant and his progress is regularly monitored, not only by probation officers or program administrators and counselors, but also by the judge. For better or worse, the judge is seen as the authority figure. Defendants do not relish having to explain to the judge why they haven't done something they were supposed to do or have done something they weren't supposed to. It is the realization that every two weeks they will be in this position, I think, that acts as a powerful motivator for many.

The flip side motivator is that it's not all bad feedback. In drug court, for example—-I presided over the juvenile drug court as one of my last assignments—those who were doing well got an attaboy and if they made it to the end there was a big deal made of it, with applause and congratulations. I am sure that for some people in these situations, it may be the first time they have had positive encouragement for anything they have done. Sad, but true. The figurative pat on the back builds pride and self-esteem and provides much-needed encouragement.

Coupling the idea of sure and swift punishment, with congratulations and words of encouragement, depending on the status, would work well, I think, for just about any other crime in which a defendant receives probation in lieu of incarceration, or even probation following incarceration. The problem is, this is a significant allotment of time for everyone involved, including the judge.

In the usual case, once you sentence a defendant they are then under the authority of the executive branch, and you don't see them again unless there is a violation of probation. If you retain jurisdiction and review the progress of each defendant on a regular basis, you are creating a lot more time in court, something usually in short supply for anyone doing felony court. And all the other players must carve out the necessary time as well. So, it's not surprising that there has not been a lot of enthusiasm for it, and the approach has been limited to certain types of crimes or populations. Perhaps, some industrious judge will convince the other players to give it a try in a more general criminal docket.

VI

The Civil Side: For Every Wrong, a Remedy

JUSTICE ON THE civil side of the law is primarily concerned with how we compensate a person for a loss suffered because of the wrongful conduct of another. This usually means an award of money (compensatory damages) though if the conduct is sufficiently egregious, there may be an award of money to punish the defendant (punitive damages.) Sometimes, where an award of damages is not an adequate remedy, the law also provides equitable remedies such as injunctions (requiring a person do something or not do something) and specific performance (requiring the person to specifically perform a contract.) An example of a case where specific performance might be required is the sale of a one-of-a-kind item. And an injunction might be the only adequate remedy for a continuing trespass on property.

Because we are not dealing with life and death, as in the criminal arena, but only with money at stake, we don't have the volume of literature and film devoted to themes of justice in civil cases. A handful come to mind: *The Verdict, A Civil Action*, and *Rainmaker*. There are a number of recent television series that portray the civil side of the practice of law, e.g., *Suits* and *The Good Fight.*

Many of the same issues we discussed related to criminal law apply to the civil side. The laws themselves should be consistent with the constitution. The procedure for resolving disputes should be fair, etc. Just as in criminal cases, we are concerned that justice delayed is justice denied, and that justice should be available to everyone, not just those with sufficient wealth to afford it. This section takes a look how those issues play out particularly in civil cases.

Both *The Verdict and Rainmaker* work with a David vs. Goliath theme. In the film, The Verdict, based on the novel by Barry Reed, a down-on-his-luck attorney, played by Paul Newman, must deal with a high-powered defense firm who is willing to cheat to win and a biased judge to win a verdict for his client in a medical malpractice case. In the final scene the jury returns a verdict in favor of the plaintiff but has a question, which I paraphrase here: "Are we limited in the award to what the plaintiff has requested? Can we award more?"

Similarly, in the film, *Rainmaker*, based on the novel by John Grisham, Matt Damon's character is fresh out of law school when he is given the case of a dying young man who is suing his insurance company for denying him coverage. He is up against a high-powered defense firm with questionable ethics who colludes with the judge to coerce a small settlement. He rejects and wins a verdict in the end—probably uncollectable as the company declares bankruptcy.

Torts

The Verdict and *Rainmaker* are tort cases. A tort is a civil wrong for which the law recognizes a legal or equitable remedy. It can be an intentional tort, such as theft, trespass, fraud, or an unintentional tort, such as negligence. An intentional tort is often also a crime. You will note several high-profile cases in which a person is charged with a crime but also sued in a civil action. Think O.J. Simpson and Bill Cosby as examples. A person can be found not guilty in a criminal case but be held liable for damages in a civil case. This is in large part because the burden of proof in a criminal case is beyond a reasonable doubt, whereas a civil claim need only be proved by the greater weight of the evidence, a much lower standard.

Negligence is generally defined as doing something a reasonably prudent person would not do, or failing to do something a reasonably prudent person would do. In laymen terms, it means being careless. If the negligence, or carelessness, is really bad, i.e., rising to a level of culpable or gross negligence, it can also be criminal. Gross negligence is doing something you know is very dangerous or risky with reckless disregard of the consequences. For example, running a red light and causing an accident would probably make you liable for negligence. Driving while very intoxicated and causing an accident would most likely make you liable for gross negligence. It could also subject you to a criminal charge.

In a civil action based on tort, a defendant is sued for damages, i.e., a sum of money that will adequately compensate the plaintiff for the injury or loss he has suffered. If it is an intentional tort, and if the conduct of the defendant is sufficiently aggravated or outrageous, a plaintiff may also recover punitive damages. As the name suggests, this would be an amount of money awarded against the defendant as punishment, in an amount sufficient to hurt the defendant financially, but not to bankrupt him.

A topic that pops up from time to time and seems popular with politicians is "tort reform." This almost always means limiting in some way a plaintiff's ability to recover damages for injuries or losses suffered because of someone's negligence. In the same breath is uttered the phrase, "frivolous lawsuits" as the evil to be remedied by this "reform." What it usually means is that some special interest (the defendant class targeted by certain lawsuits) has exerted pressure on their representatives to protect them from the financial burden of such lawsuits, and that those representatives do not trust juries to "do the right thing."

That's a shame for several reasons, but here are three:

First, every time the legislature passes such reform legislation it causes more litigation. It may be challenged as a violation of the constitution. It will have to be interpreted. This takes time and money.

Second, it is rarely effective, in part because of conflict with the constitution and because of human nature. Lawyers are trained to find ways around obstacles, to find the chink in any armor. There are almost always unanticipated and unintended consequences. For example, to address the medical malpractice "crisis" the legislature passed a law requiring the losing party to pay the attorney fees of the prevailing party. The idea was that it would discourage frivolous lawsuits.

Sounds like a good idea, but we had a law already that allowed attorney fees against a party who brought a frivolous claim or raised a frivolous defense. So, what the new medical malpractice law was aimed at were claims that weren't frivolous but were perhaps not real strong. If you got a low-ball offer to settle your suit, and you could be on the hook for the defendant's attorney fees, you might think long and hard about rejecting that offer.

The problem was the financial disparity between the parties. The doctors and other medical providers had insurance and were otherwise able to pay successful plaintiffs their damages and their attorney fees. Most plaintiffs did not have the financial ability to do so, nor insurance coverage to pay such sums. It was a one-way street in favor of plaintiffs, so it was later abandoned.

Third, I find that juries can, in fact, be trusted to do the right thing. The most talked about jury verdict, used as the prime example of jurors gone amok is the McDonald's case, in which a woman was awarded an extremely large verdict when she spilled hot coffee in her lap. On its face it does seem absurd, but when you learn all of the underlying facts, it becomes more reasonable. And, even if it wasn't, or you bring up other large verdicts that seem unreasonable, remember that the reason they make the news is because they are rare. Thousands of verdicts are rendered every year which are either zero verdicts or very much defense verdicts of a nominal sum

The current law applied to medical malpractice claims requires a plaintiff to give notice to a potential defendant of a claim, the basis for it, backed up by the affidavit of a qualified medical professional, and to give the defendant ninety days to respond and try to settle the case before suit can be filed. The idea is that cases could be mediated and settled quickly by everyone putting their cards on the table, so to speak, early on.

But again, the new law had to be challenged. It had to be interpreted. For example, what happens if a plaintiff doesn't follow the requirements to a T? Is the suit thrown out or can the defect be remedied? Requiring claimants to jump through these hoops sets up "gotcha" arguments to have a case dismissed on grounds that have nothing to do with the merits of the claim. Much time, effort and money has been spent litigating whether a plaintiff or defendant has complied with the pre-trial screening process, and if not, what is the proper remedy.

I think a better course in medical malpractice cases would be to have claims screened by a neutral panel of medical and legal experts who would evaluate a claim and give a non-binding but presumptively correct report and recommendation for resolving the case. Sort of like non-binding arbitration. You would have to work out how to select this panel so as to promote confidence by both sides that its members would not only have the expertise to evaluate the claim but could also be neutral and objective in doing so.

This would be key for two reasons: If both sides had confidence in the panel, most claims would be resolved in accordance with the findings of the panel. If not, either party could present the report as evidence at trial for the jury's consideration. I think most jurors would give such a report great weight. You could also have a provision for recovery of attorney fees by the prevailing party, but you would still have the problem mentioned above of the economic disparity of the parties.

This could be addressed by requiring the party who rejects the independent panel's recommendation to post a bond in an amount sufficient to cover costs and attorney fees of the other party if they lose in court. Yes, it would be an additional cost for some plaintiffs who could not afford it, but that is already the case for the costs of litigation, which are often advanced by the law firm representing the plaintiff anyway.

The plaintiff's attorney is often compensated by a contingency fee, meaning he or she receives a percentage, usually between 25-45 %, of the recovery. That seems like a lot, and it is, but if there is no recovery, there is no fee. The attorney may put in many, many hours of time on a case and advance a large sum of money for litigation costs, and if he or she loses the case, receive nothing for his or her services. So, they argue, the large fees in some cases compensate for those in which they receive no fee. And, in that sense, cases or claims are already screened by the attorney, who must have some confidence in the merits. Otherwise, he or she would decline to take it.

The contingency fee arrangement is not ideal, and personal injury lawyers get a lot of criticism for being "ambulance chasers" and getting rich off the misery of others. But the plain fact of the matter is that lawyers are expensive. Many people simply could not afford to pay a lawyer if billed by the hour. Even when the evidence of liability is strong, and there is little risk that a claim will be unsuccessful, the plaintiff cannot afford to pay up front, or as you go, by the hour. As a result, they end up paying a much larger fee at the end of the case. It's sort of like buying a car. If you pay cash, you pay less. If you finance the purchase, you end up paying much more.

If the lawyer takes a percentage of the recovery, the plaintiff is obviously not fully compensated for his or her loss. So, to the extent the defendant can be made to pay attorney fees, so much the better. And likewise, for defendants. If they can't recover their costs and attorney fees for successfully defending against a claim, has justice been done? If you win a case but spend more winning it than you recover, it is purely a Pyrrhic victory. So, requiring a bond be posted to cover this expense makes sense.

Some people assume that the winning party always gets their attorney fees as well. That is not the case. The law is that, unless there is a contractual provision or a statutory provision allowing recovery of attorney fees by the prevailing party, each side pays their own fees. So, without this provision, you may very well spend more in getting a judgment than you can recover.

Even when there is a provision for recovery of attorney fees, there may be a disconnect between what your lawyer charges and what is awarded to you in the case. This is because your lawyer may take a leave-no-stone-unturned, spare-no-expense approach, afraid that to do less might lead to a loss. A judge will only award a fee that is reasonable considering all the circumstances. What that means is that the prevailing party may have to pay attorney fees not recoverable from the other side.

It doesn't have to be this way, this feast or famine world of contingency fees. I'd be in favor of a universal prevailing party attorney fee arrangement, with expert screening panels as mentioned above, for all personal injury and other tort cases. If you got a favorable report, your risk of losing would be very low. And if you prevailed, the judge could take into consideration the fact that you took a risk in taking on the case, as well as the financial burden, in deciding on a fair fee. This way, the plaintiff would be fully compensated for his loss, the attorney would not get a fee disproportionate to the time and effort involved but would be fairly and adequately compensated.

Mediation

Mediation is the practice of having a neutral third-party work with both sides to negotiate an acceptable resolution of a case. This form of alternative dispute resolution began in earnest in Florida in the eighties, and it is now an established part of civil practice, required in almost all cases. Many lawyers are now full-time mediators.

It was a hard-sell at first. Lawyers complained that they were professionals and knew how to evaluate a claim and negotiate a resolution short of trial. If a case could be settled, they argued, they could settle it without the costly requirement of mediation. But the Florida Supreme Court pushed it, and lawyers grudgingly complied, and lo and behold, it worked.

Indeed, according to records kept by the Florida State Court Administrator's Office, on average, 70% of civil cases in circuit court that engage in the mediation process settle. And surveys that have been taken in Florida and across the country tell us that litigants who have a hand in the decision-making are much more satisfied with the outcome than litigants whose case has been decided by the verdict of jurors who are strangers to the case.

Arbitration

Arbitration is, like mediation, an alternative dispute resolution form. Unlike mediation, where the mediator acts as a facilitator, helping the parties reach their own agreed resolution, the arbitrator makes a ruling on the merits of the claim, very much like a judge. Arbitration can be binding or non-binding.

Many contracts require binding arbitration if there is a dispute. The theory is that it is quicker and less costly than going to court. I don't know about the less costly, since the parties pay administrative costs and the arbitrator(s) in the case which is not required by the court. But it can certainly be quicker. Another perceived benefit is that the parties choose the person(s) who will decide the case, avoiding the random selection of the judge and the perceived dice-roll involved with a jury trial. Sometimes there is a single arbitrator. Sometimes there is a panel of three arbitrators, with the plaintiff choosing one, the defendant choosing one, and those two picking the "neutral" third arbitrator.

Non-binding arbitration is typically used in a court case, with the judge referring the matter to an arbitrator to make a non-binding decision on the merits. It is intended to be a streamlined procedure with minimal testimony, if any, and relying more on written submissions by the attorneys. In essence, it gives the parties an opportunity to get an objective third party's opinion on the merits of the claim. Either party can reject the decision of the arbitrator and proceed to trial, but if they don't receive a verdict at least 25% better than the decision, they must pay the opposing party's attorney fees.

Contracts

Most people are familiar with and are touched every day by the law of contracts. It is one of the oldest, most basic concepts of the law. It is the formalization of the fundamental principles upon which cooperation is based and the foundation for a stable society. You agree to do something in "consideration" for me doing something. It could be as simple as the sale of an apple for a quarter, or as complex as the merger of two large companies, but always the motive is mutual benefit. In a capitalistic society such as ours, it is the oil that lubricates the economic engine.

The law of contracts can be deceptively simple. The general principles are intuitive and straightforward, but as with much of the law, the devil is in the details. And it is when there is disagreement as to what was intended, what was required by the language of the contract, that those details become very important. As a result, many lawyers make a good living negotiating and crafting the language of contracts. Despite the oft-used phrase, however, it is my experience that there is no such thing as "an iron-clad contract."

Well, that's a little bit of an overstatement. There are many occasions in which both parties understood what was intended by the language and one party does not perform as agreed. Try as they might, they can find no "wiggle room" to avoid liability for their "breach" of the contract because the language was precise and not subject to differences of interpretation. But that's harder to achieve than you might think.

One of the principles of contract law is that, if the language of a written contract is clear and unambiguous, it is for the court to say what it means. And neither party may offer evidence of the parties' intent, based on their conduct or their statements prior to execution of the written contract. It is like the principle of interpreting a statute, in which a court is obligated to give the language in the statute its usual and ordinary meaning, regardless of what may have been intended. Paradoxically, I often found in contract dispute cases that both sides would agree that the language under scrutiny was clear and unambiguous. However, they had completely different interpretations of what that clear and unambiguous language meant.

Sometimes the disagreement is legitimate, i.e., the parties, in good faith, disagree on what was agreed to. Sometimes, one party is in bad faith, but taking advantage of some perceived ambiguity in the language to escape responsibility. Given the nuance of our language, this is not uncommon. Parties will also use the inherent delay built into the system to delay resolution, which in turn gives them some leverage to negotiate a more favorable result. You hope that as a judge you will be able to tell which is which and enter a ruling accordingly. Again, it is easier said than done.

I found that in business, most parties will make an economic decision rather than one based on what is legally correct. This often means that the faultless party to a contract will accept less than they are entitled to under the contract to avoid the delay and expense of litigation. And remember, just as we discussed above in tort cases, even if there is a provision for the recovery of attorney fees by the prevailing party, there is no guarantee that you will recover the full fee paid. A litigant will naturally have to ask himself if it is worth the delay and expense to go forward.

This may offend our sense of justice, but it is no different than the fluid, rough justice that results from plea negotiations in criminal cases. It is the same principle at work in civil cases. Unless you can find a way to make litigation available with little or no cost to the litigant and can reach a final, enforceable judgment reasonably quickly, this rough justice will continue to be an integral part of the resolution of disputes because it is more efficient.

Real Property Law and Wills and Probate

When we talk about property, we distinguish between personal property, such as cars and clothes, and real property, which refers to a legal interest in land or something affixed to the land. Any former law students reading this are probably recalling, fondly, or not so fondly, those hypotheticals about "Blackacre" and the bundle of rights associated with various forms of title: fee simple, tenants in common, tenants with right of survivorship, tenants by the entirety, life estate, leasehold, easement, lien, license, etc.

I will not bore you with a definition or explanation of the various interests one may have in real property, or the myriad legal requirements for passing that interest upon your death. Suffice it to say that, in a country such as ours, which is based on the concept of private property, this area of the law is very important to the orderly function of our society and economy. As with contract law, the law of real property, and of wills and probate, rely upon preciseness in language and adherence to certain formal, procedural requirements that can be a trap for the unwary.

As a result, lawyers are reluctant to stray from the archaic language that has been used to convey interests in real property for centuries. The reasoning is, we know how this language has been interpreted in the past. If we change it, we can't be sure how it will be interpreted if a dispute arises. The downside is that conciseness is often a victim of this reliance on archaic language, as illustrated by the following:

One day in Contract Law class, Professor Jepson asked one of his better students, "Now if you were to give someone an orange, how would you go about it?" The student replied, "Here's an orange." The professor was livid. "No! No! Think like a lawyer!"

The student then recited, "Okay, I'd tell him, 'I hereby give and convey to you all and singular, my estate and interests, rights, claim, title, and advantages of and in, said orange, together with all its rind, juice, pulp, and seeds, and all rights and advantages with full power to bite, cut, freeze and otherwise eat the same, or give the same away with and without the pulp, juice, rind and seeds, anything herein before or hereinafter or in any deed, or deeds, instruments of whatever nature or kind whatsoever to the contrary in anywise notwithstanding..."

You get the idea. It's why some people claim lawyers think they are paid by the word. A lot of the redundancy in the language used in wills, and deeds, and other related documents dates back to the convergence of the French language with the Old English in the eleventh century, after the Norman conquest. Legal documents, to make sure everyone understood what was meant, began using such doublets as cease and desist, have and to hold, devise and bequeath, etc., synonyms from the different languages.

I have long been a proponent of getting rid of legalese and jargon to the extent possible in favor of plain language that your ordinary layperson can understand. There has been improvement in many areas but the law in general, and in these areas specifically, values stability and certainty. People need to know what to expect and need to rely on enduring principles to govern their conduct.

The law is conservative by nature and change comes slowly, which in general is a good thing, though often results in inefficiencies that are frustrating and seem to have no good reason other than lining the pockets of lawyers or feeding an ever-increasing government bureaucracy. Anyone who has ever bought or sold a house knows what I am talking about. So, instead of simplifying the process, we seem to be making it more and more complex. More law, less justice!

Family Law

If there was ever an area of the law not well-served by the adversary system, it is family law, which includes divorce, with issues of parental responsibility and parenting time (what used to be called child custody and visitation) and child support, and division of property. We should probably add to this mix juvenile dependency cases, in which it is determined that a child is dependent upon the state for services because of the failure of the parents to provide them. And if you are going to include dependency cases under the family law umbrella, you might as well also include juvenile delinquency cases, because there is often a correlation, if not a causation between the two. A delinquent child often turns out to be a dependent child as well, and vice versa.

Marriage is a form of contract. Both parties promise to be faithful to each other for the rest of their lives, to love and cherish each other in sickness and in health, and whether they are poor or rich, or somewhere in between. Sometimes these marriage vows are supplemented by what is called a pre-nuptial agreement, which gets very specific about what is expected, and especially what will happen in the event the marriage is dissolved. I always thought such agreements were very unromantic and pessimistic or cynical, almost a jinx to the marriage before it gets started. It says in effect, I don't trust you, or me, or both. I must admit, however, that, given the current odds against any marriage lasting until one spouse dies, it is very practical.

At any rate, as with any other contract, a party to a marriage may not live up to his or her agreement. Under Florida law, you can decide you don't want to love and cherish your spouse any longer, and get the marriage dissolved. You can do this whether your spouse has done anything bad or has not been keeping the marriage vows. In fact, you can be the one who was unfaithful, or mistreated your spouse, or otherwise did not honor your vows. It doesn't matter. You don't have to have a reason to divorce your spouse, other than you want to.

In Florida, we call this "no-fault" divorce. What that means is that, legally, we don't care who is at "fault" for the breakup. We will settle the joint property and decide matters of child custody and support without regard to who is to "blame" for the dissolution of the marriage. As an aside, "dissolution" is the legal term for what most people call divorce—another example of unnecessary complication in the law.

This "no-fault" concept is very unsatisfying to the spouse who perceives himself or herself to be the injured party. They want the court to punish the other spouse for their wickedness and cruelty. They want affirmation that they are the virtuous one. They want to vent about the other's misdeeds and failings. And they consider it unfair if they're not allowed to. A little venting serves a useful purpose in most disputes, and especially in family law cases. Whether it is legally relevant or not, and it usually isn't, it is psychologically important for the litigant.

It may be enough to vent to the lawyer, who can explain, sympathetically, that while he understands what a total jerk the other spouse is, legally it can't be presented as evidence at trial. And it doesn't hurt for the judge to deliver that message again if a spouse begins to go down that road. And, in fact, in many divorce and other family law cases, the parties do not have lawyers—can't afford one—so no one has explained this to them. I find that allowing a little venting on both sides, but also explaining the legal concept of no-fault divorce, goes a long way toward making them feel as if they have been heard, and they understand why you cannot let them turn the trial into a therapy session.

Many judges hate being assigned to the Family Law Division. I remember one colleague remarking that he'd rather do a capital murder trial than a hotly contested divorce. It can be emotionally trying, especially when you are dealing with children, and the venom each spouse spews against the other. You can get frustrated dealing with people who can't even agree on how to divide the pots and pans. All in all, it can test your patience. I never minded it, though, either as a lawyer or a judge. In fact, it is an area in which you can help people through a bad time, help lower the temperature in the room, so to speak. You get to play a little Dr. Phil occasionally, as in "How's that working out for you?" to point out the obvious folly of a path of conduct someone has traveled with the expected adverse consequences.

As in all areas of the law, the statutes and the rules have gotten more voluminous over the years, and the discretion of the judge has been whittled away with requirements of written orders considering certain factors. You know how I feel about more and more complicated laws, but there is a good side to this, at least good intentions. It makes the judge think about and articulate the factors the Legislature thought important in matters like child custody, for example, or what to do when a couple divorces and custody and visitation has been worked out, but then one spouse wants to move far away.

If you want to get really depressed, though, take a turn in dependency court. You deal with dysfunctional families, parents who are drug addicts or just plain sorry parents who neglect or abuse their children. Most of the time, they have good intentions but lack the ability to do better, or perhaps the will.

The stated goal when the Department of Children and Family Services intervenes in a family is to reunite parents with children, or to provide services to make it unnecessary to remove them in the first place. It's a difficult road for parents as they have to make their way to counselors, jump through all sorts of hoops to get the government out of their business. On the other hand, the department is overworked and underfunded and must deal with parents who are frustrated and frustrating.

You must remember that, try as we might, we have never been able to come up with a good substitute for two stable, loving parents in bringing up healthy, moral, and productive citizens. So, we must do our best to keep the family intact. Sometimes, it just doesn't work. We can't wait forever for parents to get their act together, and if they can't, we must find some alternative, permanent arrangement for the kids. We end up terminating the legal rights of the parents. That can be a tough situation for everybody, including the judge.

When I was first on the bench, as a county judge, I was assigned to dependency, covering for the circuit judge who normally handles this docket. I had not done dependency cases as a lawyer, so I had a bit of a learning curve. Fortunately, the "regulars" helped me understand what had to be done and I settled into the job. I ended up with a termination of parental rights case right off the bat.

Most of these cases, I later learned from experience, are usually not contested. By the time it reaches this point the parents have been given all kinds of chances to come through and get their act together. But my luck, new in the division, I get a fiercely contested one. It took five days to try and there were five children involved. There were several issues but probably the key one was whether the mother's boyfriend was physically and sexually abusive to one or more of the children and the case hinged on the testimony of a young child.

The thing about dependency, a judge really needs at least a basic knowledge about child development if you really want to understand what's best for a child, and what to expect of children, depending on their ages. So, I did some outside reading to get up to speed.

It was a tough decision, but I ended up denying the request to terminate the rights of the mother. I certainly had my doubts and there were certainly many concerns. But, applying the law and considering the burden of proof (clear and convincing evidence,) I found the department had not proven its case. I knew these kids were going to have the deck stacked against them. And sure enough, some years later, when I did juvenile delinquency cases, and adult felony cases, they were regular customers.

VII

In the Eye of the Beholder: Law as Protector or Oppressor

Rich and Poor

Winter's Bone

IN THE RURAL Ozarks of Missouri, seventeen-year-old Ree Dolly looks after her mentally ill mother, twelve-year-old brother, Sonny, and six-year-old sister, Ashlee. She makes sure her siblings eat and teaches them survival skills such as hunting and cooking. The family is destitute. Ree's father, Jessup, has not been home for a long time; his whereabouts are unknown. He is out on bail following an arrest for manufacturing meth.

Sheriff Baskin tells Ree that if her father does not appear for his court date, they will lose the house because it was put up as part of his bond. Ree sets out to find her father. She starts with her meth-addicted uncle, Teardrop, and continues to more distant kin, eventually trying to talk to the local crime boss, Thump Milton. Milton refuses to see her; the only information Ree comes up with are warnings to leave the situation alone and stories that Jessup died in a meth lab fire or skipped town to avoid the trial.

When Jessup fails to appear for the trial, the bondsman comes looking for him and tells Ree that she has about a week before the house and land are seized. Ree tells him that Jessup must be dead, because "Dollys don't run." He tells her that she must provide proof that her father is dead to avoid the bond being forfeited.

Ree tries to go see Milton again and is severely beaten by the women of his family. Teardrop rescues Ree, promising her attackers that she will not cause more trouble. Teardrop tells Ree that her father was killed because he was going to inform on other meth cookers, but he does not know who killed him. He warns her that if she finds out who did, she must not tell him.

A few nights later, the Milton women who beat Ree come to her house and offer to take her to "[her] daddy's bones". The women place a sack on her head and drive her to a pond, where they row to a shallow area in which her father's submerged body lies. They tell Ree to reach into the water and grasp her father's hands so they can cut them off with a chainsaw; the severed arms will serve as proof of death for the authorities.

Ree later takes the hands to the sheriff, telling him that someone flung them onto the porch of her house. The bondsman gives Ree the cash portion of the bond, which was put up by an anonymous associate of Jessup.

This is a very harsh world of poverty and crime. Both the movie and the novel by Daniel Woodrell on which it is based do a great job of portraying its reality. Ree, played by Jennifer Lawrence, is fiercely independent, and proud. "Don't ask for what ought to be offered," she tells her little brother. She also has dogged determination. She makes no boasts, issues no threats, but just keeps going after what she needs. This is a dangerous trait under the circumstances, but one which makes you want to root for her. In her father's world, everyone is a criminal, depends on a criminal, or sells to criminals. That they are engaging in illegal activities makes them vulnerable to informers and plea-bargainers, so they are understandably suspicious, even of family members. Family is strong but the code is stronger. "Family gets a little thin…"

There is a similarity to *The Godfather* here, where family is central, but loyalty is demanded of everyone, including family. If you will recall, Michael has his own brother, Fredo, killed because he betrayed the Family. He broke the code of loyalty. And in Ree's world, as in the Godfather's, violence is a moral, integral part of justice. "You was warned once, nice like…."

In *The Ox Bow Incident*, not only is the law portrayed as slow and ineffective, but it is also actively oppressive, antagonistic to the interests of the regular person. From their perspective, the law protected those "plush-bottomed, soft-handed bastards, who couldn't even drive their own wagons." This is a common perspective, reflected in our stories and films, and a real-life perception of how justice, or injustice, is meted out, based upon your wealth, or lack thereof.

This is natural, inescapable perhaps, in our capitalistic society. Money means power, and those who have it, have power. The laws enacted, and enforced, serve those with the money and the power. It's not that straightforward, of course, as those in power can act altruistically. They can realize and acknowledge the benefit of even-handed application of the law. But it is unlikely that they will give up the advantage that their wealth gives them.

One of the most satisfying story closures is when the high and mighty are shown to not be above the law. In the film, *And Justice for All*, Al Pacino's character, a lawyer, is coerced into representing an arrogant judge who is accused of rape. In his opening statement, he tells the jury that the prosecutor is going to try and tap into their emotion that says, let's get someone in power. Let's get a judge.

This emotion runs strong through our collective psyche. We like to think, as Atticus Finch says in *To Kill a Mockingbird,* that our courts are the great levelers, that everyone is equal before the law. And I think we strive to make this a reality, understanding that we fall short. It's why I didn't like to let a defendant pay out his community service hours but would let someone convert fines and court costs to community service hours, even if they could afford it. My thought was that everybody was better off with community service.

Black and White

O.J. Simpson and A Few Good Men Revisited

How do we explain the very different reactions to the verdict in the OJ Simpson case? At the time, polls indicated that 87% of Whites thought OJ was guilty, but only 27% of Blacks thought he was guilty. And this was the trial of the century, watched by millions of people on their televisions. How could people viewing the same evidence see it so differently?

I think it's inescapable that the race of the defendant and his lead attorney was the most important factor. I think a lot of Blacks at the time told themselves that the man was innocent, but they didn't really believe it. Another more recent poll in 2016 indicated that the percentage of African Americans who believed in his guilt went from 27% to 57%. Pundits and others who analyzed the case had their theories, but nobody could really escape the race factor. The prevailing view goes something like this:

Many, from experience, saw an incredibly racist criminal justice system. The man was framed. It was all about Mark Fuhrman and planting evidence. Even those who thought he was probably guilty still liked the verdict. This was bigger than O.J. It was about their life experiences and the whole experience of African Americans with the criminal justice system. Those Black women on the jury were the mothers, the wives, the sisters, and the girlfriends of Black men who had been mistreated by the police. They were open to the potential argument that the police might in fact plant evidence or lie against someone accused of a serious crime.

Perhaps it had to do with Johnnie Cochran, a man of color commanding that courtroom, beating the system, a Black, brilliant attorney winning the case against all the odds. A further delicious irony for many African Americans was that the vindication against the system was with a black man that White America loved, a black man White America thought was not like others of his race. He wasn't a troublemaker. He upheld their values. He didn't cause racial consternation. He wasn't controversial. For many African Americans this was sticking it in the eye of the Man. And it felt good. It felt fair.

There is no question in my mind that the perception of justice in general and often in particular cases is heavily influenced by your race. This is borne out in conversations or statements on the news or talk shows or comments on social media or the results of polls. This is especially true as to the difference between the perception of justice by Whites and Blacks, though I think it also holds for other races.

Given the long history of slavery in this country and the subsequent widespread oppressive treatment of former slaves and their descendants, it is no wonder that many people of color often consider the law not as a protector but as an oppressor. This is especially true for those charged with enforcing the law. These people have a lot of discretion as to who is stopped on the street, who is arrested, and who is charged. From personal experience or from what they are told from family and friends, many African Americans often distrust the motives and intentions of law enforcement. They also lack confidence that the "system" will treat them fairly in determining guilt or innocence. And if found guilty, they fear they will be sentenced more harshly than a White defendant in a similar situation.

Many feel like they live on Orwell's *Animal Farm*, where some animals are more equal than others. If you are rich or White, especially if you are rich *and* White, there is a different justice system for you. If you are poor, or a person of color, especially if you are both, it's a whole 'nother story. It's one of the biggest challenges for the system itself, and the folks that run it. We want to think that the people making decisions all along the way are operating from good faith, trying their best to perform their duty objectively and even-handedly. The perception in some quarters, however, is that racial bias, implicit and explicit, affects all these decisions, that the entire criminal justice system is afflicted with institutional racism from top to bottom.

Those who work in the criminal justice system bristle at these accusations, aware that injustices may occur but certain that they do their best every day to be fair to everyone and don't have a racist bone in their body. They argue that if there are more people of color charged and convicted of crimes, it is because they are the ones committing the crimes, and that many of the victims of those crimes are people of color.

The truth, as usual, is probably somewhere in between. Things are rarely black and white (pun intended) but are more nuanced than some would like to think. Certainly, it is a bit ironic that those who complain about stereotyping by police tend to paint all within the system with the same brush. Whatever the reality may be, the perception is that some defendants are treated differently because of their race. Many African Americans and other people of color don't trust the police. That's why the different reaction to the OJ Simpson verdict.

And unfortunately, unless you have been living under a rock, you have heard witness accounts and have seen cell phone video footage of incidents that support this perception, e.g., George Floyd. And every time that is shown to be the case, trust and confidence in the fairness and justness of the system suffers. That's why it is critically important that we take a good hard look at every aspect of the criminal justice system and do what is necessary to promote confidence that people will be treated fairly.

The experience of most White people is quite different, and the perception much different. For the most part, they see the law and those who enforce it as protectors rather than oppressors. They rarely have been harassed or mistreated by a police officer, nor know of family or close friends who have. They are more likely to be strong law and order supporters, willing to give law enforcement the benefit of doubt if someone claims abuse. As we discussed in *A Few Good Men*, many agree with Colonel Jessup *that in places you don't talk about at parties, you want me on that wall. You need me on that wall. ... You rise and sleep under the blanket of freedom I provide and question the manner in which I provide it. I'd rather you just said thank you.*

Every time a cellphone video captures police excessive use of force it becomes more difficult to turn a blind eye, and it reinforces the perception that there is a different justice for you if you are a person of color. Of course, perception is not necessarily reality in many cases. Just because you are a person of color doesn't mean that you were wrongfully charged, wrongfully convicted, and given an unfair sentence because of your skin color. Your skin color is not an excuse.

If the goal is building public trust and confidence in the justice system, though, I think it requires acknowledgment of the reality of historical mistreatment and discriminatory enforcement of the law against people of color and the resultant perception by a large percentage of the population that the law is not protective but rather oppressive. Transparency and candor are important tools in building trust and confidence, as is constant evaluation of process and decisions.

Pro se Litigants

DUI Santa

The Defendant was wearing a Santa cap on Christmas eve when he was pulled over for erratic driving. The officer suspected the man was under the influence, a suspicion heightened after a brief encounter with Santa and his inability to adequately perform a variety of field sobriety exercises. When the officer advised the defendant that he was going to be arrested, he objected, verbally and physically. He had to be subdued and, as a result, was charged with DUI and resisting an officer with violence, the latter being a felony.

The defendant maintained his innocence of both crimes, and claimed he was severely injured because of police brutality. Indeed, he declared his plan to sue the city for the injuries he received. He came to court in a wheelchair because he said he couldn't walk. Unfortunately for him, the encounter was recorded on the dash cam of the patrol vehicle. To the objective observer it confirmed the officer's version of the event.

The defendant, however, was not an objective observer. In fact, it soon became obvious that he had only the barest grasp on reality. His attorney filed a motion to determine his competency. He was found incompetent and sent to Florida State Hospital for treatment and competency restoration.

When he was later found competent and returned to the jail, he remained insistent that he wanted a trial. Despite his lawyer's advice, he would not accept a plea offer for time served. It was unlikely that he would receive more time than he had already served if he was found guilty, but by the time his trial came around, he would have served at least another couple of months.

He also created additional delays by his own actions. He accused his lawyer of sleeping with the prosecutor and conspiring against him and sought to have him replaced. When that failed, he sought to discharge his attorney and represent himself. Then he would change his mind and want his attorney back. He seemed to enjoy the attention.

What made this case, and this defendant, different from other obstructionist defendants, was his artistic bent. Specifically, he liked to illustrate his motions and arguments with cartoon drawings. They were actually a bit humorous, though also biting. As they say, a picture is worth a thousand words.

Well, eventually, he had his trial, and to no surprise to anyone besides the defendant, he was found guilty. It took the jury about twenty minutes to come to their verdict. At sentencing, given that he had been in jail pretrial for two years, he figured I would give him time served. I decided, however, that he needed supervision to keep him stable, and out of trouble. This surprised him and made him quite angry. As he was wheeled out that last time in his wheelchair, he reiterated his intention to appeal, and to sue the city for his injuries.

Some months later, I signed a warrant for his arrest for violation of his probation. I don't remember exactly what he had done or hadn't done, but I don't think it was based on a new law violation. When he appeared in court to answer the charge, in his wheelchair again, I read the arrest report which stated that when the officer went to his house to arrest him, he could see the defendant standing in the kitchen area, apparently washing dishes. When the officer announced his identity and purpose, the defendant took off through the back door and started running. The officer chased him for about a hundred yards before catching and subduing him. I had to suppress a smile.

Sovereign Citizen

Self-described "sovereign citizens" see themselves as a law unto themselves, answerable only to their particular interpretation of the common law and not subject to any government authority. They do not recognize United States currency. They reject most forms of taxation as illegitimate. Indeed, they claim that the United States government, and state governments as well, are for the most part illegitimate. They believe that the county sheriff is the most powerful law-enforcement officer in the country, with authority superior to that of any federal agent, elected official, or local law-enforcement official. This belief is shared with other extremist groups like Posse Comitatus and the Constitutional Militia Movement.

Their philosophy is a mishmash of common law and uniform commercial code nonsense. They will often file liens against government officials who have done something against them. They will demand that the judge answer a number of questions that go to the supposed lack of authority. It never pays to try to have a rational discussion with them as they are not rational. The FBI considers some sovereign citizens, the extremists, to be domestic terrorists, utilizing violence to achieve their ends. In surveys conducted in 2014 and 2015, representatives of US law enforcement ranked the risk of terrorism from the sovereign-citizen movement higher than the risk from any other group, including Islamic extremism, militias, racists, and Neo-Nazis.

Some are hard-core sovereign believers, and dangerous. Some are newbies who adopt and test sovereign techniques for resisting everything from speeding tickets to drug and other charges. I've had several, mostly of the latter category. One particular defendant I remember took this approach much to his disadvantage. He was charged with multiple burglaries and had an extensive record, mostly thefts and burglaries. He seemed pretty normal early on but soon began to act in a way that fit the profile of a sovereign citizen. While he was out on bond, he made several written threats against officials, which resulted in new criminal charges and a revocation of his bond on the pending charges.

He refused his court appointed lawyer and decided to represent himself. It's never a good idea, but everybody has a constitutional right to self-representation. The only requirement is that the decision be a knowing one. The judge thus does an extensive colloquy (a discussion with and advisory to the defendant) to determine that he, with full knowledge of the disadvantages, still wants to represent himself. The disadvantages are numerous and obvious—a lawyer is trained in procedure and evidence, and you are not, just to mention one big one. As with many sovereigns, and other arrogant defendants who think they are the smartest person in the room, the defendant, despite being advised of all the disadvantages, elected to represent himself. It turned out to be a very bad decision.

The first case to go to trial was a burglary of a residence during a power outage after a very bad storm. The key witness for the State was an elderly woman who lived next door to the home that was burglarized. She testified to seeing a man parked in her neighbor's driveway. She watched as he removed items from the storage shed attached to the carport and placed them in his vehicle. She called police but the man had gone by the time they arrived.

Sometime later, the man returned, this time to her house. From inside, she saw him peering in her front window. Instead of cowering in a corner and calling 911, she opened her front door and yelled out, "What are you doing here?"

"I was checking to see if you need any tree service," the man said.

"I don't have any trees in my living room. You didn't think anybody was home, did you? Now get out of here."

The man left in a hurry. The woman called the police again, gave them a description of the man and the vehicle, which matched that of the defendant when he was arrested several days later. Several stolen items were also found in the vehicle. At trial, the spunky neighbor, we'll call her Ms. Smith, identified the defendant as the man she saw that day. The defendant's cross-examination of the witness was one foot-in-mouth blunder after another:

"Now, Ms. Smith, are you sure that the man you saw was the defendant?" (Pro se defendants often refer to themselves in the third person, which always seems weird to me, and a little ridiculous.)

"Yes."

"In your description," he says, looking at the paper in his hand, "you said the man had a receding hairline."

"Yeah, like yours."

"Well, I don't think I have a receding hairline."

But he did.

"And you said his hair was light brown."

"Yes, like yours."

"But my hair is dark brown, isn't it?"

"No. It's light brown."

"Well, I guess the jury will decide that."

It was clearly light brown.

A similar question and answer about his height followed and then he sprang for what he must have thought was the coup de grace. "And you described the man's accent as from New Jersey, right?"

"Yes."

With a knowing look to the jury, "Well, I'm from Louisiana." You could almost hear the 'aha' in his voice.

The witness shrugged. "Well, it sounds like New Jersey to me."

And it did.

It took a very short time for the jury to return a verdict of guilty. The defendant, his grip on reality still very precarious, was shocked. He was also shocked at sentencing when I gave him a stiff sentence, justified, I thought, by the extensive record he had. I thought maybe the guilty verdict and the significant sentence would bring him back to the world of rational thought, and that he might abandon his dabbling in the sovereign citizen approach. But he remained consistent in his denial of the court's authority and, under protest, continued to represent himself. When I rotated out of the division, he had been convicted at least one more time and was awaiting trial on several other charges.

A Fish Story

I presided over a lot of interesting cases in county court. This one is a good example of the occasional impressive creativity of the pro se litigant. The defendant had been charged with two fishing violations—taking too many fish in a single day and too many in a three-day period. Not the most serious case, you might say, but I can assure you that this litigant, indeed, most litigants in county court, took their case very seriously.

The defendant wanted to suppress the evidence obtained because of a search of his house, specifically a whole lot of fish. I denied the motion. The search had been pursuant to a search warrant, which meant that another judge had already determined that there was probable cause to believe evidence of a crime would be found.

So, we tried the case. The evidence against him was compelling on the three-day charge. I don't remember what the limit was, but he had way more than was allowed in his house. On the charge of exceeding the limit in a single day, the wildlife officer testified that he observed the defendant going out on the lake in his boat with an empty cooler, and when he returned later in the day, he had considerably more fish than the law allowed. The defendant maintained that his cooler was half full from the day before, so the total was not unlawful.

When the defendant cross-examined the officer, he asked him how he could be sure that some of the fish weren't already in the cooler from the day before. The officer said because he watched the cooler as he accelerated away from the dock and it was jiggling and bouncing around with the motion of the boat, indicating it was light, and not weighed down with fish as it had been when he returned.

The defendant had the officer indicate on a diagram of the fish camp where his boat was and where the officer was standing when he observed him going out on the lake. When it was his turn to present evidence, the defendant asked if he could show me a video he and his friend had produced.

"What does it show?" I asked.

"I put my friend with the video camera in the spot the officer says he was standing, and I drove my boat out from the same place on the dock, and I put my empty cooler in the bottom of the boat where the officer says it was. I want you to see whether the cooler moves around like he said it did."

So, I agreed he could play it. The video showed the defendant putting his empty cooler in the boat, then getting in his boat and pulling away from the dock. I watched as the boat slowly moved out of view.

"Did you see that cooler bumping around on the deck, Judge?"

"I couldn't see the cooler at all," I said.

"Exactly," he exclaimed.

I found him not guilty of the charge.

Hot Button Topics

If you feel very passionate about an issue, have very strong opinions about it, you are likely to be far on the just result end of the ends vs means scale. Only if you get the result you wanted was justice done. This is often true on hot button issues like abortion. I had my share of controversial cases with local, regional and nation-wide audiences that showcased this principle. Let's look at some and see if you agree or disagree with the result and consider why.

Challenges to the constitutionality of legislation in Florida almost always end up in Circuit Court in Tallahassee, as the state has its principal offices here and enjoys a statutory "home" venue privilege. This is why Governor Lawton Chiles is reputed to have remarked that if he was to be a judge, he would want to be a circuit judge in Tallahassee, because you heard cases that no other circuit heard. I agree. I would have enjoyed being a circuit judge anywhere in the state, but I've always preferred variety, and circuit court in Tallahassee offered a whole separate category of cases I would not have been exposed to otherwise.

Sometimes, when I was assigned one of the more difficult cases, I might have had second thoughts about that proposition, but not for long. We might kid about it but I think that most of us want to be challenged, to be tested. As was commonly observed among judges, tongue firmly in cheek, "That's why they pay us the big bucks." It wasn't long after my appointment to the circuit bench that I was assigned one of those "big bucks" cases.

Abortion: Parental Notification

In 1989, the Florida Supreme Court declared unconstitutional a statute that required parental *consent* for a minor to have an abortion. The primary basis for the opinion was the provision in the Florida state constitution granting a right of privacy to its citizens, basically telling the government to stay out of our personal lives. Ten years later, the Legislature passed a similar statute that required a parent be *notified* if a minor child sought an abortion. This statute was also challenged as being a violation of the privacy provision of Florida's constitution. It was assigned to me.

Of course, anything to do with abortion stirs up passions and brings news media coverage. The case went to a non-jury trial, which lasted about three days. When it was done, I felt that the factual dispute had really been more a difference of opinion. I took the matter under advisement. It was close to a holiday as I recall, Thanksgiving or Christmas.

Like most cases in which people have an interest, the ends versus means scale generally tipped towards the ends side, with most people concerned only with the result, and not a lot about the integrity of how you got there. If you are pro-choice, you want the statute declared unconstitutional. If you are against abortion, you want it upheld. You might want to see some strong language in the order that confirms your view, that sticks it in the eye of those on the other side, but mostly you just want the result.

If you are somewhere in the middle. If you have views on the matter but realize that good people may have differing views, you are okay with some sort of legal answer. You are open to a decision that is arrived at by a good faith analysis of the law and application of that law to the facts as found from the evidence. It is the tried-and-true method we have relied on since we've had the rule of law. It depends, of course, on the integrity of the person making the decision.

People tend to think a judge's decision on the law reflects their personal belief or feeling on the issue. This is true regardless of what is said or written by the judge explaining his or her decision. The truth of it is that your personal feeling about it is irrelevant. This is why the judicial rules on ethics prohibit judges or judicial candidates from expressing their personal opinion on any issue that might later come before them. You don't want to say something that suggests you might be less than impartial and objective on a particular issue.

It may make it more difficult to rule in a case when your individual moral code conflicts with your professional duty, but you have to make the ruling the law and the evidence requires, as best you can determine it. If you can't do that, if you can't be objective and impartial because of your feelings or views on the issue or the parties, you are required to recuse yourself, i.e., get off the case and let someone else decide it.

Of course, if you have to do this on a regular basis, recuse yourself, then you shouldn't be a judge. You end up passing the buck, and the burden of decision, to your colleagues—which itself is not fair. One of my colleagues used to joke that he could be fair and neutral on any case because, "I'm pretty much ambivalent about everything."

One of the fundamental principles I operated under as a judge was that I should always explain my decision, either orally or in writing. I thought it important that the litigants understand how I got to the final result. They may not agree, but the hope is that they understand and accept that my different view was arrived at logically and in good faith.

In this case, I decided that the 1989 Florida Supreme Court case on parental consent pretty much controlled this case and dictated how I should rule, i.e., that the law violated the privacy provision in the Florida Constitution. While notification was less of a restriction than consent, as a practical matter the result would be the same, as the parent could use their authority and influence to coerce their child to make the decision they wanted.

Sure, you might say, that's what parents do. You want to be informed of any important event or condition affecting your child's physical or mental health. You want to be there for them, to support and comfort them. Being a parent myself, I was sympathetic to this view. But not every parent will be supportive and comforting. And though there is a difference in degree from consent and notification, the rationale on which the 1989 case was based was applicable here as well, and I was bound by that precedent.

Those who liked the result were pleased and felt justice was done. Those who didn't were sure justice was not done, and that some judge was thwarting the will of the people as expressed through their representatives. Of course, the Florida Constitution trumps any law passed by the Legislature, and is the expressed will of the people, and I felt my ruling was consistent with that constitution. The case was appealed to the First District Court of Appeal, which reversed me, and eventually to the Florida Supreme Court, which reversed the DCA and upheld my ruling.

Interestingly, I had noted in my ruling that what the proponents of the law could have done is seek to have the right to privacy provision in the constitution amended to make an exception for minors. And they did, a few years later. Now, parents must be notified if their minor child seeks an abortion—though there is a procedure the minor can follow to seek a waiver if she has a good reason why she doesn't want to tell her parents, e.g., physical abuse.

Bush v Gore

This was my 15 minutes of fame, I guess, at least for news junkies caught up in the drama of the post-election legal wrangling in 2000. It's been almost 25 years now, so a lot of people have no memory of it at all and for many, the memory of it has faded considerably. It was a big news story for a while, until 9/11. There was a pretty large cast in the drama and my role was fairly minor, but because I had the first case filed in the capital, and was tasked with handling the state-wide recount, it will probably be an asterisk or footnote mentioned in my obituary—which I hope is not necessary for several more years.

Election night, I was at the Tallahassee Bar meeting awaiting election results. I was talking with Marshall Cassedy Sr., who was Director of the Florida Bar and a dear man. He said to me, "You know, Terry, I think this election is going to be so close, we're not going to know who the winner is tonight."

I then gave what was the first of my many incorrect predictions about this election. "Oh, I don't think so, Marshall. I mean, it will probably be really close, but they have voting machines now that are quick, efficient and accurate. It'll be close but we'll know who the winner is fairly soon after the polls close."

Not!

A day or so later, lawyers in Palm Beach County were complaining about butterfly ballots and were making requests under the election code for a recount of certain precincts. Someone asked me if I thought we would get any of those protest cases in Tallahassee, and I said, "No, that's all down there in south Florida. We had no problem with voting machines here."

Must the Secretary of State Count Late Vote Results? A couple of days later, Volusia County, followed quickly by Dade and Broward counties, filed a complaint in Leon County against the Secretary of State for Declaratory Judgment and Injunction. A declaratory judgment is a remedy available when you have a dispute with another person or entity as to the interpretation of a law, a contract, or some other document. You are asking for a declaration as to the rights and obligations of the parties to the suit so as to avoid anticipated harm. An injunction is an equitable remedy often coupled with the declaratory relief sought, asking the judge to enjoin, i.e., to order that the other party do something or not do something.

In this case, the counties had sent word to the Secretary, whose duties included overseeing all statewide elections, that a request for recounts of certain precincts might put them beyond the date they were required to certify their results to the secretary, i.e., seven days after the election. The secretary had told the counties, in essence, too bad. If they didn't get their votes in on time, they would not be counted.

The counties wanted me to "declare" that their interpretation of the pertinent election law was accurate and that the Secretary of State was wrong in telling them the votes would not be counted if they were late. They wanted me to tell her that she must accept the returns after they did their recounts.

There were two statutory provisions in play. One part of the law did require, as the secretary maintained, that counties certify their election results no later than seven days from election day. The use of the word "shall" in this law meant it was mandatory. The other provision provided that the secretary "may" reject results that were not timely certified and filed with the secretary.

I ruled that the use of the term "may" instead of "shall" in this latter provision, meant that the secretary could, in fact, accept late filed returns, if she so chose. In other words, she had discretion in the matter. And, to say ahead of time that she would not count the votes if they were late was an abdication of that duty to exercise discretion.

There might be any number of legitimate reasons why the counties could not comply with the statutory requirement, reasons why it would be reasonable for the secretary to accept late filed returns. I gave a few examples: Hurricane or other natural catastrophe, failure of equipment, loss of electricity. She needed to consider the reason before she could exercise her sound discretion in the matter.

Both sides saw something positive in the ruling. Gore's folks saw it as an admonishment to the secretary, a declaration that she had been wrong to insist on timely filed returns. The Bush folks took comfort in the fact that I didn't grant the relief requested, i.e., to tell the secretary she had to accept the late filed returns. I thought, on the whole, that it was favorable to the counties, because the secretary had said she wasn't going to count them, period, and now she was required to at least consider the reasons and attending circumstances. I thought it would be at least several days before it came back to me, if at all, because it was going to take a few days for the counties to finish their re-counts, and then the secretary would have to decide whether to count them or not.

I was wrong, again, with this prediction.

The more cynical among you might point out that the secretary was also the campaign chair for George Bush in Florida, and her guy was ahead. If those questioned precincts were recounted, they were democratic leaning and there was no reason to believe it would help Bush, only hurt. Besides, why take the chance? On the other hand, the Gore supporters were not seeking a recount of all the votes, only those in precincts that leaned democratic, probably hoping that the lead would change to favor Gore and Bush would be the one having to file a full election challenge and ask for a state-wide re-count.

You might also be thinking that the secretary, afraid that a recount in the heavy democratic precincts would put Gore ahead of Bush, would figure out a way to exercise her discretion, as I had said she must, without waiting to see what the results were. It would certainly look worse if she declined to accept them after a recount showed Gore ahead.

I'm not cynical by nature, and I have no way of knowing what she was thinking, but she found a way. She quickly sent a letter to the counties asking them to tell her why they felt they couldn't get the returns in by the required date. She then considered their answers and declared they were not good enough reasons and said late-filed returns would not be counted.

Predictably, the counties came running back to court, asking me to find the secretary in contempt for not following my order. She had jumped the gun, they said, not waiting for the re-count and deciding ahead of time that the circumstances did not justify accepting the late-filed returns. She had abused her discretion, they said. It was all a pretext; she was never going to consider counting them. The secretary said she had done just what I ordered, considered the attending circumstances behind the delay and exercised her discretion in denying the request for an extension of time. Well, as I said, I didn't, and don't, know what her motivation was, but in the context of my previous rulings, it didn't matter.

My order was short and to the point. The secretary had been required to consider the circumstances surrounding the late-filed returns in exercising her discretion as to whether she would accept or reject them. It was not for me to tell her what she must decide. If the counties or the candidates felt she had abused her discretion in not allowing extra time in doing a recount, there was a remedy for that. That is, it might be grounds for an election contest.

My ruling did not mean that I agreed with the secretary's decision, but rather only that she had done what I ordered and was not in contempt as the counties argued. The Gore folks decided to appeal to the Florida Supreme Court. I think I understand why. They wanted to get ahead in the vote count and thought the contested counties in south Florida would do it for them and put the Bush team in the position of having to contest the election. Much better optics. They were already contending with "Sore Loser" signs.

But I thought then, and now, that it was a mistake. I wouldn't have worried about the optics. Like I said, they already had that. If I had been the Gore team, I would have come back to me with an amended complaint, contesting the election and asking for a state-wide manual re-count—which is where they ended up anyway, but after wasting precious time on appeals and other suits. By the time they had the election contest and the appeal to the Florida Supreme Court, they were running quickly out of time.

A note here about the time element. In most local and state-wide elections, a contest of an election might take months, even years to resolve. If the challenge is successful, the challenger takes office then and finishes out the term. Not so for presidential elections. Under the U.S. Constitution, and federal statutes, each state has to certify their electors for the electoral college by a certain date.

With this deadline looming, the Florida Supreme Court heard oral arguments on the Gore team's appeal. And I believe because of the time limitations, they did something appellate courts generally do not do. They, in essence, determined that the secretary had abused her discretion, but instead of sending it back to me for further proceedings to determine a proper remedy, they extended the time for the counties to file their returns.

This was unusual because there was no record evidence to suggest what time would be necessary or reasonable. I had offered the parties an opportunity to do just that in the second hearing, to establish a record, but they declined. Perhaps they weren't prepared to do so. I recall that one of the justices, Major Harding, asked during oral argument how the justices were supposed to determine a date, just pull it out of the air? My sentiment exactly.

Nevertheless, the Court chose the Sunday after Thanksgiving, as I recall, as of 5:00 pm, if the secretary was open for business on that day, and if not, the following Monday. This coincided with the deadline for receiving military or overseas ballots. The secretary, of course, decided to open on that Sunday and when the counties were not quite able to get the returns in before the deadline, rejected them and certified the election in favor of Bush. So, the appeal to the Florida Supreme Court by the Gore team was for naught, and a good bit of time was spent to get to where it was headed anyway, a general contest of the election.

This election contest case was randomly assigned to Sandy Sauls, another Circuit Court judge, who conducted the trial over a period of three weeks. I watched some of it as it was broadcast live on television, but it was rather tedious, and I had other cases to work on, one of which was election related.

Martin and Seminole Counties. Judge Nikki Clark was assigned a case claiming fraud and other election law violations in Seminole County concerning absentee ballots. Unlike the election contest which focused on 900 ballots in Dade County, this claim involved a couple thousand votes. Depending on her ruling, this had far more potential to change the election results. I remember going by her office and opining just that, that she had the sleeper case, the one getting the least attention but with the most potential to affect the results.

Then, a couple of days later, I got a case out of Martin County, with the same factual and legal issues, and involving a large number of ballots. I talked with Judge Clark and we agreed to do our independent research and analysis, but to confer before entering final orders. It was important, we thought, that we reach the same conclusion, if we could, for consistency's sake. And if not, at least we would know why and how to address our differences in our orders. We also wanted to issue the orders at the same time as well. As it turned out we came to the same conclusion independently, specifically, that while there may have been some law violations, they did not result in fraudulent votes, and to void those votes now would not be a proper remedy.

Election Contest/Recount. The election contest case concluded and Sauls ruled against the Gore folks, saying a state-wide recount was not required. They appealed to the Florida Supreme Court, which, in a 50-page opinion, reversed

Sauls and remanded the case to him to conduct a state-wide recount. The order came out late on Friday afternoon. It was either the trial court administrator or the chief judge, who came to my office with a copy of the opinion and reported that Judge Sauls had recused himself from further participation in the case. The normal rotation would then have put Judge Clark on the case, but she was out of pocket and unable to take the case. She had also had a particularly bad week as the target of cruel, racist comments and death threats. Did I have any reason I couldn't handle it? No, I did not.

I had also received hundreds of emails, letters and cards, some rather nasty, but nothing like Judge Clark had received. Some called me a hero, a patriot, an American stallion. Some called me a coward, and corrupt. One person said he hoped I burned in Hell, and had a long miserable life before then. I think the responses were motivated by the result of my rulings. If they liked it, I was a patriot, if not, I was a traitor. One lawyer from New York actually looked at the issues and the process and understood what I did and why. That was refreshing. My favorite, though, was a postcard from a woman in Tennessee, who started out, "You are one handsome man."

I read the Florida Supreme Court's opinion over carefully. The bottom line was that I was expected to supervise a state-wide manual recount. The court seemed concerned that some voting machines registered a "no" vote because the voter had not sufficiently shaded in the ballot or punched through the ballot, but that an examination of the ballot itself may very well show the voter's "clear intent" as to their vote, and thus should be counted. There were no specific directions as to how to do the re-count and, consistent with previous opinions, no specific direction as to how to determine the "clear intent" of the voter. At the time, there was some variation from county to county as to what criteria to apply, e.g., the hanging chad versus the dimpled chad.

I asked court administration to contact all of our local judges and see if they would be willing to come in to consult as to the best way to carry out the Florida Supreme Court's order, and to volunteer to come in the next day to count the ballots from Dade County. Several judges responded and came to my office. There was some discussion, some differences of opinion and advice, which I appreciated. One judge suggested that I needed to establish uniform standards or criteria for examining the ballots, without which, the re-count was doomed. As it turned out, he was right, but I didn't think I had the authority to specify to the canvassing boards how they were to count the ballots or give any other guidance other than as provided in the election law, i.e., to determine "the clear intent of the voter."

The contested ballots from Dade County had been brought to Leon County for the election contest trial, so those would be counted locally, and I figured having judges do the counting would give the public more confidence in the fairness and objectivity of the count. Similarly, I planned to ask my fellow judges in the other counties, starting with the chief judges of each circuit, to take an active role in insuring a fair and orderly process in each county. Of course, the canvassing boards in each county had a county judge as one of its members by law. I hoped and believed that by including judges in the process the partisan bickering could be minimized. For similar reasons, and for efficiency, I decided that representatives of the parties could be present for the re-counts but could not make contemporaneous objections to the process or to any individual ballot decision. Any argument would be made to me, after the fact, and I would resolve any disputes.

After I had a plan in mind and my notes on it, I scheduled a conference with the attorneys to get their input. The Gore team was in favor of just about anything that would result in a quick re-count because unless and until it was done and the result changed, they had lost. The Bush team, on the other hand, wanted to be able to contest each individual ballot at the source. They also wanted me to give the canvassing boards specific instructions as to how to determine if ballots were to be counted. While I sympathized with this latter request, the desire to have uniform standards to apply, I noted that the Florida Supreme Court had been asked, twice, to do so but had declined. Rather, I said, we were limited to what was in the statute, "the clear intent of the voter," and I was not free to re-write the law.

One of the questions I have been asked in interviews and conversations about this case is whether there was anything I regretted about how I ruled or handled things. Generally, second thoughts or regrets in this job as judge will paralyze you and give you sleepless nights. You have to make the best decision you can, then move on. Doesn't mean you were right, and you should learn from your mistakes, but you can't dwell on it. I will say that when I discussed the procedure with the attorneys and the Bush team complained about the lack of uniform standards, I later wished I had addressed this argument in more detail. As it turned out it seemed to be one of the main issues the U.S. Supreme Court latched onto in their order stopping the re-count, saying the different standards resulted in a denial of equal protection.

I know it's the highest court in the land, and I know they were dealing with something some said was a constitutional crisis, but I never could see this argument. In hindsight, maybe I could have addressed this at the time. It might not have made a bit of difference, but it would have been consistent with my general policy of explaining my ruling. While it was true that the Florida Supreme Court had not set any specific criteria or standards for re-counting the ballots when asked, and although that was reason enough for me not to do it, there was also a logical, legally principled reason why this was not a valid argument against going forward with only the statutory direction to determine, if you could, "the clear intent of the voter."

To the argument that this was too general and vague, I would point out that every day in this state jurors are asked to judge whether a person is guilty of serious crimes based on "reasonable doubt," and to award large sums of money in civil cases if they find that a defendant was "negligent." The definitions of these two terms are the height of vagueness and generality. Consider:

A reasonable doubt is not a mere possible doubt, a speculative, imaginary or forced doubt. Such a doubt must not influence you to return a verdict of not guilty if you have an abiding conviction of guilt. On the other hand, if, after carefully considering, comparing and weighing all the evidence, there is not an abiding conviction of guilt, or, if, having a conviction, it is one which is not stable but one which wavers and vacillates, then the charge is not proved beyond every reasonable doubt and you must find the defendant not guilty because the doubt is reasonable.

And:

Negligence is the failure to use reasonable care, which is the care that a reasonably careful person would use under like circumstances. Negligence is doing something that a reasonably careful person would not do under like circumstances or failing to do something that a reasonably careful person would do under like circumstances.

Based on these instructions, it is quite possible, even likely, that two juries, with similar facts might reach opposite conclusions as to guilt or innocence, or negligence. We are, after all, dealing with human beings and very human processes. But we don't say it is a denial of equal protection because of the different results. Frankly, we are loath to know what goes on inside the jury room, how they apply those vague and general instructions (laws and sausages, you know) but it seems to work fairly well most of the time. To ask the canvassing board to count a ballot if they can determine "the clear intent of the voter" is no more of an equal protection violation than it is to ask jurors to determine guilt based on whether they have a "reasonable doubt." The term is no more vague.

If I was to give any direction, I would have chosen a "Johnny Cochran" phrase my wife, Fran, came up with: "If in doubt, toss it out." It certainly would have made a good sound bite. And it actually sums up about the only advice I could have given in my opinion. If you couldn't readily tell, from looking at the ballot, that the voter intended to vote for a particular candidate, then it shouldn't be counted. There is nothing in the law that requires that, though, so I didn't order it. There are three persons on the canvassing board, Hopefully, all three should agree. But, in the event that there lurks some implicit or explicit partisan bias that keeps them from being completely objective, I was to be the one to make a final determination.

Anyway, there we were, getting close to midnight that Friday at a management conference with the attorneys, with world-wide news media coverage, and I set out the procedure I would follow to comply with the Florida Supreme Court's mandate for the re-count. And I make the request of my fellow judges around the state to become involved in their respective circuits, and assuming they are all following the case, I ask that the canvassing boards fax to me the protocol they establish for the recount. As was mentioned to me afterward, I gave the whole world who was watching it on television my fax number, inviting all the crackpots out there to fax me. True. Not a good move on my part, and I was surprised we didn't get more prank faxes. And yes, we were still using fax machines then.

Of course, many of my colleagues suggested I had missed a golden opportunity to promote my novel. I had written and had published a legal thriller called *Conflict of Interest*. All I had to do, I was told, was to prop it up on the bench where the camera would pick it up. Yuk, yuk.

Co-incidentally, I actually did get a very favorable, perhaps inadvertent, review by a columnist with the Baltimore Sun. A friend sent me a copy. This was right after my second ruling in the case against Secretary Harris, in which I ruled she had not violated my order. The columnist praised my ruling as an example of integrity amongst the partisan squabbling. He had read in the background information on me that I had penned a novel, a legal thriller. Then he proceeded to praise the writing, concluding that I had a fine eye and ear, and that whatever I did as a judge he hoped I would continue writing.

I came in early the next morning, Saturday, and reviewed the faxes and other communications from election officials. Ron Labasky, attorney for the association of supervisors of election, helped coordinate communications, and Ion Sancho, our local supervisor of elections, helped coordinate the local counting of ballots from Dade County. Several local judges volunteered to do the manual re-count.

It appeared that almost all of the canvassing boards had set up plans and protocols to conduct a re-count and felt they could have the results by the deadline I had given of mid-afternoon on Sunday. Only one county, Duval, expressed concern about their ability to complete a re-count by the deadline, but I remained optimistic, and figured I would contact the chief judge there if problems could not be resolved. It seemed that it was a matter of politics rather than resources. There was one county that wanted to know by what authority I was ordering a re-count. I referred them to the order from the Florida Supreme Court, which I attached. They responded that they would comply.

One county, Okaloosa, wanted to know whether they were to count "over votes" as well as "no votes." The opinion from the Florida Supreme Court talked a lot about "no votes," in which the machine registered no vote because the punch card wasn't punched hard enough, etc., but nothing about ballots that were rejected by the machine because the voter had marked more than one candidate. I didn't see any difference. The question was whether the clear intent of the voter could be determined. In the example I was given from Okaloosa County, the ballot was one by which a voter filled in a line next to the candidate. This particular voter had filled it in for both Bush and the Libertarian candidate (whose name escapes me) but had "Xed through the line for the Libertarian candidate. It seemed obvious that the clear intent of the voter was to vote for George Bush, and that is what I said in response to the inquiry.

I had set the deadline with the calculation that it would give me time to consider any objections from the litigants, resolve any factual disputes about the ballots, give a final tally and enter a final order, declaring the winner. Again, I would be assisted by our local supervisor of election and my fellow judges. I planned to rule as quickly as possible to allow as much time as possible for appeals. As it turned out, the re-count didn't last that long.

By late morning, I received word that the Federal Circuit Court had agreed to review the appeal from the Bush team and didn't want us to enter judgment until they had a chance to consider it. Shortly thereafter, I received word via CNN that the U.S. Supreme Court had taken the case and ordered the re-count to cease until it ruled.

Well, that pretty much signaled what was going to happen. There was no reason to stop the re-count if you weren't sure how you were going to rule. They were going to declare that Bush was president-elect. And they didn't want the authority of the decision to be adversely affected by a re-count that showed Gore with more votes than Bush. That would be more than awkward.

The only question was what legal basis they would use to justify their decision. As I hinted earlier, the central basis seemed to be a determination that because of the lack of specific criteria to examine the ballots to determine the clear intent of the voter, and the different criteria utilized by different canvassing boards, there was a violation of both equal protection and due process. You already know my opinion on that. I didn't buy it then and I don't buy it now. Apparently, the Court didn't think much of it either as they expressly stated that it was not to be considered of precedential value in any future case.

Now, that tells you a lot. What an extraordinary statement about an opinion from the highest court in the land. In fairness, they probably thought they were doing what was necessary to avoid a constitutional crisis, afraid of the chaos and unrest that might result if they didn't shut down the re-count. I hope not as that seems rather patronizing, showing a lack of faith in the people and the institutions of our government. It's hard for me to second guess them, though, as I was not there and don't know what was discussed. And reasonable persons can disagree. All I know is that I didn't agree with the reasoning or the decision to stop the re-count.

The next day, Sunday, I was taking a walk with my wife and she asked me whether I was disappointed or glad that I had not had to make a final ruling. Part of me was relieved that I didn't have to make the decision, which was sure to be controversial either way, but especially if the results showed Gore as the winner. And there is always a concern that you will blow it, that you will make a decision that is widely seen as wrong on the law, unfair, or in some way makes you look like a fool, and in front of a very large audience.

So sure, part of me was relieved, but it was a small part. I was more disappointed than relieved. It may sound strange but one of the most satisfying things about being a judge was the challenge of a difficult case, of having to make the difficult decision. As I have mentioned, a judge needs to be both humble and confident. Humble in the knowledge that you are fallible, but confident in your sense of fairness and your ability to make a fair and legal decision. Someone has to do it, so it might as well be you.

As a citizen, I wanted to know, and probably most people wanted to know if a manual re-count of the ballots rejected by voting machines would change the result, i.e., show Gore had actually received more votes than Bush. There was no reason, no legal reason, for the Supreme Court to stop the manual re-count. If the Court decided the results shouldn't be counted, then so be it, but as a factual matter, shouldn't we know? As I speculated above, I think the Court was afraid that if the manual re-count showed Gore the winner, the decision to not recognize it would lack credibility, even more than it did as it was.

A collection of news organizations conducted their own unofficial re-count with inconclusive results. As I remember it, if you took the approach advocated by the Gore team, a more liberal view of which ballots could be counted, Bush still won. If you took the approach advocated by the Bush team, a more restrictive view of what could be counted, Gore would have won. I guess we'll never know what an official tally would have shown.

I've given interviews, spoken to classes, participated in forums and otherwise talked to people about the 2000 election litigation and my role in it. That is why, perhaps, I can remember a good bit of it. Then again, one's memory of an event changes they say, every time you retrieve it.

Some overall impressions: This seems to have opened the floodgates for election litigation. What used to be seen as tacky or definitely un-statesman-like, is now an accepted part of any campaign. And arguably, it was the beginning of the deepening partisan divide in the country. The two go together. The more divided, the closer the vote, the more likely a contest of the initial results in court. You could see the partisanship play out in 2000 with the talking heads speculating on what I or some other judge was likely to do based on our party affiliation or that of the governor who appointed us.

That was hogwash, of course. But just as pathological liars assume that everybody lies, so too diehard partisans see the world through that lens and assume everyone has a political agenda. That's behind the increased emphasis and strategy in appointment of judges. It also seemed to me that the Bush team and supporters were quick to criticize judges and accuse them of improper political decisions. They were strident and abusive and helped, I think, to undermine trust and confidence in our institutions, specifically the courts. For the most part, Gore's team and supporters were respectful of the process and the decisions of the various courts while still advocating their position. Gore was gracious in his acceptance of the Supreme Court's ruling.

Fast forward twenty years to the election of 2020 and its aftermath, and we see how far that partisan extremism has been extended. The level of political discord and lack of civility in our politics is higher than any time in my lifetime. And as in 2000, it has been lopsided on the side of the Republicans, just much worse.

You already know my views on this from our ends v means discussion earlier. And unlike in 2000, where the margin of victory was paper thin (537 votes in Florida), Trump lost by thousands of votes in the key states. And, unlike Gore's gracious concession when he lost in court, Donald Trump never conceded. He was the antithesis of the gracious loser. Whether his massive ego could not accept that he had lost, or he knew he had and didn't care, he should have accepted the rulings of the court and conceded.

I am well-aware that many of you will dismiss my observation as deluded, as just plain wrong – because it doesn't agree with your viewpoint. Not trying to convince you. Just explaining how I see the partisanship and lack of respect for our institutions on display in 2020 has morphed into something truly frightening. And many of our so-called political leaders have sat on their hands and buttoned up their mouths and stood idly by while this has happened. What a lack of leadership and statesmanship.

As I write this, the presidential election of 2024 has concluded and Donald Trump has been declared the winner. Surprisingly enough, despite the dire warnings of Trump and his camp, there was apparently no wide-spread fraud in this election, no irregularities. Why? Because he won.

And importantly, there were no cries from the Harris team or her supporters of a stolen election, of wide-spread fraud. Only a gracious concession speech from Kamala Harris. The contrast with the reaction of Trump four years earlier was stark.

Abortion and Medicaid; Waiting Period for Abortion

The issue of abortion came before me a few more times during my time on the circuit bench. In one case, plaintiffs filed suit seeking a declaration that refusing to provide Medicaid funds for abortion procedures violated the Florida and U.S. constitutions. The essence of the argument was that it discriminated against poor women, who couldn't afford to pay for the procedure. I agreed that it discriminated against poor women and it wasn't fair, but had to conclude that it wasn't illegal or unconstitutional. The case law pretty much told me that one had a right to have an abortion, but couldn't require the government to pay for it. This ruling was upheld on appeal.

Later, towards the end of my time on the bench, the Legislature passed a law requiring a waiting period after an initial visit to a doctor, and a subsequent visit to a doctor, before a woman could get an abortion. In general, this was similar to the situation in the parental notification case. In both, the state defended the statute in part on the grounds that, because of the physical and psychological risks to patients in having an abortion, it was medically appropriate to impose a waiting period to make sure women understood the risks of what they were doing.

The problem with this argument was that the facts did not support it. Specifically, in no other medical procedure, even those much riskier than an abortion and fraught with possible psychological trauma or later regret, did the state require a waiting period. Such disparate treatment belied the suggested "compelling state interest" advanced in argument. Moreover, if the Legislature seeks to limit a constitutional right, it is required to do so in the least restrictive means possible. Here, the statute was an across-the-board, broad-sweeping requirement that made no distinction based on any circumstances.

My judgment in the case was reversed by the First District Court of Appeal after I left the court, but the DCA was later reversed by the Florida Supreme Court and the ruling upheld. And again, I suspect that many people weren't too interested in how I came to the decision, the rationale for it. They were only concerned with the result.

That's to be expected in hot button or controversial cases. All you can hope for is that those with an open mind will consider the rationale behind the decision, the explanation of how it was reached. And even if it was not the result they wanted, they can accept that the result is based on a good faith application of the law to the facts.

The Leon High Case

A tradition at a local high school was for the students to put out an underground newspaper at the end of the year which made fun of teachers and administrators, allowing the students to vent a bit, I guess. It was, also by tradition, a tasteless collection of diatribes. This time, one of the targets, a teacher, thought they crossed the line. The teacher sued the students involved for intentional infliction of emotional distress.

The case came to me on summary judgment motions from the students involved. The facts weren't really in dispute. The question was whether what the students had written met the legal requirements for a claim of intentional infliction of emotional distress. In order to recover on a such a claim, the plaintiff must prove four elements:

1. The defendant's behavior must be so extreme that it goes beyond what is acceptable.

2. The defendant must have acted intentionally to cause distress or with reckless disregard for the possibility of causing distress.

3. The emotional distress suffered must be significant and debilitating enough to negatively affect mental health.

4. The defendant's action caused the emotional distress.

I found for the defendants that, as a matter of law, the cruel and hurtful things written in the newspaper were not sufficient to support the plaintiff's claim. I thought the conduct of the students was "outrageous" but, in my view, the case law did not support a cause of action by the teacher. The First District Court of Appeal disagreed and reversed me, ruling that the Plaintiff could proceed with her claim.

Of course, as a trial judge, I never liked to be reversed by the appellate court. But I also realized that reasonable people could disagree with an interpretation of the law. What you didn't want to see as a trial judge was an opinion reversing you that started with something like... *As we have said many times before*.... Here, it didn't really hurt my feelings too much as I thought it was a close call anyway. The case didn't go further as it was settled shortly thereafter.

Missed Deadline

The owner and manager of a local restaurant in Tallahassee was a popular county commissioner who was up for re-election. Somehow, the deadline for qualifying for office came and went without him filing the necessary documents and paying the filing fee. It was an apparent oversight on his part, as he had every intention of running. When the Supervisor of Elections refused to accept his late-filed papers, he sued. The case was assigned to me.

I was not personal friends with the man but our professional relationship was cordial, and I thought he had done a good job of representing his constituents. Unfortunately, the law on the subject was, in my opinion, clearly against him. The statute on qualifying for office was very strict. If you didn't timely file the required paperwork and pay the filing fee, you couldn't run for the office. Period.

He complained that he was the incumbent, and everybody knew he was going to seek re-election, including the Supervisor of Elections, who should have given him a heads up as the deadline approached. None of that, however, was a legal excuse for not complying with the qualification statute, and so I ruled against him. The ruling was affirmed on appeal.

The public reaction was mixed, judging by letters to the local newspaper and to me personally. Some thought the Supervisor of Elections had intentionally sandbagged him. Others observed that he was not entitled to special treatment because he was the incumbent, and suggested his failure to keep up with the paperwork did not speak well of his ability to do the job he sought. His wife expressed her displeasure with my ruling by returning to me the copy of my novel, *Conflict of Interest*, she had purchased for her husband, with a suggestion for a title for my next one, "How I Stole the Vote from the Citizens."

All these cases are examples of how reasonable people can differ greatly in their perception of whether justice has been done because of their strong, passionate opinion about an issue. You can only hope that they are handled in such a manner that even if they disagree with the result, they can accept it as a good faith disagreement as to what the law requires.

As I approached 2018, I had to decide whether to run for another term. If re-elected, I would be 67 years old when I began the new term. The Florida Constitution provided that a judge must retire from active service upon reaching the age of 70—unless you were half-way through your term, in which event you could serve two more years. We often referred to this provision as "constitutional senility."

My birthday is in December, so I would be just short of half-way when I turned 70. There was a proposed constitutional amendment to increase the mandatory retirement age to 75, which of course would allow me to serve a full term, and maybe a little more. It was a tough call. I loved the job. But I would have been at it for almost 30 years. I didn't feel like burn-out was a problem, but I didn't want it to become one either. Fran had been retired for a few years and there were things we wanted to do that weren't possible if I was working full-time. We also had two young grandchildren with whom I wanted to spend more time. And I would have more time to write. In the end I decided not to run for another term.

My last term had its share of interesting, compelling, and sometimes high-profile cases, and I continued to learn and to struggle with the notions of justice we have discussed in this book. The most high-profile and controversial of the cases during my last term was the fight over reapportionment of congressional seats after the 2010 census.

Redistricting

Talk about diehard partisanship!

Because of a Supreme Court case in 1964, states are required to apportion their congressional districts so that they have the same number of voters, based on the most recent census, the one man-one vote principle. If they are not equal, it dilutes the voters in the district with more voters. And based on the ruling, the population in one district cannot vary from another by more than one or two votes. Which is rather arbitrary since the population shifts and changes daily, and by the time the districts are drawn, it is unlikely that the populations have remained the same. But, that is what the law requires.

After each census, the states draw up new congressional districts, apportioning their populations accordingly. Historically, the political party in power has drawn the district lines so as to give their party, or some group, or incumbents, an advantage. In other words, the officeholders pick their voters rather than the other way around. As a result, the apportionment map may have district lines that curve all over the place, like a bizarre jig saw puzzle. The process and the result are referred to as gerrymandering.

The term, gerrymandering, was used for the first time in a Boston newspaper in 1812, in reaction to a redrawing of Massachusetts state senate election districts under Governor Elbridge Gerry that redistricted Massachusetts to benefit his Democratic-Republican Party. When mapped, one of the contorted districts in the Boston area was said to resemble the shape of a mythological salamander. Gerrymander was thus a portmanteau of the governor's last name and the word salamander.

Two principal tactics are used in gerrymandering: "cracking" (i.e. diluting the voting power of the opposing party's supporters across many districts) and "packing" (concentrating the opposing party's voting power in one district to reduce their voting power in other districts). In addition to its use achieving desired electoral results for a particular party, gerrymandering may be used to help or hinder a particular demographic, such as a political, ethnic, racial, linguistic, religious, or class group. As the result of court orders, some federal voting districts have been gerrymandered so as to produce a sufficient percentage of African-American or other racial minorities to presumably carry the district. These are called "majority-minority districts".

In 2010, the voters in Florida approved an amendment to the state constitution which was intended to curb these gerrymandering abuses. It forbade drawing districts with the intent to favor incumbents or a political party, or to disfavor a minority racial group. The state legislature drew up apportionment maps for the state senate and house districts and for the congressional districts. The maps were immediately challenged in court by The League of Women Voters and others. The case challenging the congressional map was assigned to me.

By its nature, litigation concerning apportionment only comes up in Florida every ten years, after the census (although as I write this, Texas and other republican controlled states are planning to redraw congressional maps mid-decade in a blatantly partisan move to retain control of the house. California and other democratic controlled states are threatening to do the same if they do.) At any rate, while lawyers might develop expertise by handling cases in different jurisdictions, it would be difficult for a judge to gain any such specialized knowledge or expertise. I had no experience in this area of the law, either as a lawyer or a judge.

The law in this area is complicated enough, but the technical terms used to describe the process of mapping and the corresponding analysis required in assessing whether the map complies with the required criteria, presented real challenges for this non-stem-oriented judge. Fortunately, I had the assistance of one of our law clerks who had an interest in and aptitude for the subject.

Speaking of law clerks—we called them staff attorneys—it always seemed backwards to me that the trial judges, who had to make many more decisions than the appellate courts, and much quicker, got a pool of staff attorneys (roughly one per five judges) while each appellate judge got one to three law clerks specifically assigned to them, in addition to a pool of law clerks to assist in researching and writing opinions. For many fewer cases, and with greater time to do so. Not that I'm complaining....

The case was hotly contested. There were numerous discovery disputes, motions to dismiss and for summary judgment. There were multiple appeals of my pre-trial rulings, and a three-day trial. We were working with a brand-new constitutional amendment that had to be interpreted. And there was pressure to reach a decision quickly, well before the next election. In other words, just the type of interesting, challenging case I liked to handle.

In the end, I found that the map drawn by the legislature was in violation of the new "Fair Districts" constitutional amendment. Specifically, I found that Republican operatives, disguising their identity, and through the guise of citizen input during public hearings, had surreptitiously presented proposed maps that favored Republican incumbents and candidates. Those maps somehow ended up being the source for the end-product of the Legislature.

The cynical approach by the partisans to side-step the law in an effort to maintain political power brought to mind words from the farewell address of President George Washington as he left office, which I quoted in part in the beginning of my Final Judgment:

However combinations or associations of the above description [parties or factions] may now and then answer popular ends, they are likely, in the course of time and things, to become potent engines by which cunning, ambitious, and unprincipled men will be enabled to subvert the power of the people and to usurp for themselves the reins of government, destroying afterwards the very engines which have lifted them to unjust dominion....

The alternate domination of one faction over another, sharpened by the spirit of revenge natural to party dissension, which in different ages and countries has perpetrated the most horrid enormities, is itself a frightful despotism. But this leads at length to a more formal and permanent despotism. The disorders and miseries which result gradually incline the minds of men to seek security and repose in the absolute power of an individual; and sooner or later the chief of some prevailing faction, more able or more fortunate than his competitors, turns this disposition to the purposes of his own elevation on the ruins of public liberty.

These words seemed very prophetic when I wrote my order, and even more so today.

I spent about three and a half years in Franklin County, where I handled everything—civil, family, probate and guardianship, juvenile dependency and delinquency, and criminal. Although I always liked to have a variety of cases, it is difficult to stay on top of all areas of the law from day to day. Fortunately, I had lawyers and clerks to help me keep up. Although it required me to travel and stay overnight on a regular basis, I liked the assignment, and the small town (Apalachicola) and the people I worked with. There was no shortage of interesting litigants and cases in Franklin County with issues of law and justice. Here are a few:

Stand Your Ground Revisited

One of the first cases I presided over in Franklin County was a criminal case in which the defendant had struck his brother with his fist, causing him to fall and strike his head, resulting in his death. It happened in a bar and the whole thing was recorded on video. The defendant filed a motion to bar the prosecution under the "stand your ground" law. His argument was that the brother had become quite intoxicated and was harassing and threatening other patrons, specifically including his girlfriend and another male. So, to protect these third persons the defendant walked up to his brother and cold-cocked him.

The law does allow you to use deadly force in defense of third persons, and the same factual issues are in play. Did the defendant have a right to be where he was? Did he have a reasonable fear that the person was about to commit a forcible felony against the third person? Was the use of deadly force reasonably necessary to prevent the forcible felony?

Having watched the video and listened to the testimony, I thought the brother was, in fact, a threat to his girlfriend and the other person. Although the defendant gave him a "sucker punch" of sorts, as he came up on the side and gave no warning before swinging, I thought it was reasonable on the part of the defendant. Specifically, one does not usually consider hitting someone on the side of the head to be "deadly force." At most you would think he might be knocked unconscious. Apparently, he hit his head on the foot railing of the bar on his way down and that's what killed him. It was really kind of a freak accident.

I thus ruled that the defendant had acted in self-defense (of third persons) and granted the motion to dismiss. I noted that the defendant would have to live with the guilt of having killed his own brother, which would be its own special punishment, but further prosecution by the state was not warranted.

Rainbow Family

Later, I had another stand your ground case in which the defendant was charged with murder and attempted murder. By this time the Legislature had amended the statute again, this time to provide that if a defendant filed a motion to dismiss or to bar prosecution based on self-defense, the state would have the burden of proving, by clear and convincing evidence, that self-defense was not applicable. The initial legal question to be resolved was whether the amended statute applied prospectively or retroactively. If it applied prospectively, the defendant had the burden of proving his motion by the greater weight of the evidence. If it applied retroactively, the state would have the burden to refute the claim of self-defense by clear and convincing evidence.

This legal issue had yet to be resolved with any finality by any Florida appellate court. Various circuit courts throughout the state which had considered the issue had come to different conclusions. The judges in my circuit who had considered the issue had each ruled that it applied prospectively only, and I decided to remain consistent with those rulings. Because of the uncertainty in the law, however, and with the anticipation that whatever ruling I made might be appealed, and to eliminate the necessity of a new hearing if I was wrong, I declared that I would also determine whether the state had met the clear and convincing evidence burden.

The defendant and the victims were all members or participants to some degree in a group known as the Rainbow Family. This group gathers and camps for weeks at a time in national forests throughout the country. On March 5, 2015, the group was camping in a national forest located in Franklin County, in an area known as Wrights Lake. During the early morning hours of March 5, 2015, the defendant shot and killed Jacob Cardwell. He shot and paralyzed, but did not kill, Wesley Jones. He claimed he was acting in self-defense.

The defendant and Wesley Jones offered somewhat consistent but critically contradictory narratives of how Mr. Jones ended up being shot by the defendant. According to the defendant, he confronted some people who were burning a tire, which was not allowed in a national forest. The confrontation escalated with Jones attacking him with a shovel as he was trying to retreat. When Jones hit him in the face with the shovel, defendant shot three times. According to Jones, it was the defendant who pointed a gun at him first. When he tried to push the gun away with a folding shovel, the defendant shot him. There were internal inconsistencies in the defendant's testimony that led me to find that the he had not met his burden of proving by the greater weight of the evidence that he was justified in the use of deadly force against Wesley Jones.

For similar reasons, I found he had also failed to meet this burden as to Jacob Cardwell. Defendant testified that he was leaning against his trailer, attempting to collect himself after the trauma of having shot Jones when Cardwell came at him with a machete, and he shot him two times. Cardwell was unable to dispute this testimony as he was killed by the defendant, but the defendant's version was directly contradicted by the testimony of other witnesses, including Jones.

And, even accepting the defendant's testimony that Cardwell came at him with a machete, that didn't mean he was justified in using deadly force. Admittedly, if someone is coming at you with a machete, it is understandable that you would shoot them to protect yourself from harm. But a precondition to the lawful use of deadly force is that you are lawfully where you have a right to be and are not otherwise engaged in criminal activity.

Pointing a gun at someone is an aggravated assault. Shooting them is at least aggravated battery. If you commit two violent felonies and appear capable of committing more violence, you don't get to kill someone who tries to stop you, and then claim self-defense. And if the testimony of Jones and the others was to be believed, that is what happened. Given the disputed evidence and inconsistencies in defendant's version, I found he had not met his burden, assuming the amended statute applied prospectively.

If the amended statute was found to be applied retroactively, however, I found that the State had not met its burden as to either Jones or Cardwell, as there were also some inconsistencies in their testimony as well. There is a big difference between the defendant persuading me by the greater weight of the evidence that he acted in lawful self-defense and the State persuading me by clear and convincing evidence that he did not. Not only did the burden shift under the revised statute, the burden of proof was considerably higher.

Clear and convincing evidence is evidence that is precise, explicit, lacking in confusion, and of such weight that it produces a firm belief or conviction without hesitation about the matter in issue. The evidence must be credible; the memories of the witnesses must be clear and without confusion; and the sum total of the evidence must be of sufficient weight to convince the trier of fact without hesitancy.

I noted that reasonable people could differ on this and, ironically, if the matter was before me on a motion for directed verdict at trial based on the evidence presented, I might very well deny it. That is because I must give every reasonable inference in favor of the State. The jury is free to believe or disbelieve all or any part of the evidence, and reasonable people could disagree on what the evidence proved. But as the fact-finder on the defendant's motion, I just couldn't say that the evidence was clear and convincing.

My order was appealed and the District Court of Appeal ruled that the amended law was to be applied retroactively, and thus, based on my findings in the order, the case was sent back for entry of an order granting the motion. I don't know if the Florida Supreme Court has decided the issue yet, or even if the state appealed.

My feelings about the "stand your ground" statute have not changed. I think it was ill-advised for the reasons outlined in my first order after its initial passage, and the amendment shifting and raising the burden of proof standard has just made it worse. It encourages violence instead of discouraging it, as the previous law did. It places machismo over human life, allowing people to instigate a confrontation and then resort to deadly force when it could have been avoided. It gives no protection to innocent persons caught in the crossfire of a gang shootout, so long as someone can claim self-defense, even if they are reckless in their self-defense.

And it creates an administrative nightmare. Before the amendment, self-defense was an affirmative defense a defendant could raise in a trial. Now, all the defendant has to do is file a motion and the state must present to a judge, pre-trial, sufficient evidence to refute a claim of self-defense by clear and convincing evidence. And, if the motion is not granted and the case proceeds to trial, the same witnesses will have to testify twice. There will, in effect, be two trials. As if courts didn't have enough to do.

Moreover, if there are several co-defendants—as there were in my gang shootout case—you may have several motions and hearings, one for each defendant. You might be able to hear all of them at the same time, but not if all defendants have not yet filed a motion. More time required of judge, lawyers, witnesses and other court staff. And you run the risk of having different, contradictory results based on the evidence presented, or not, at each hearing, or the skill of the different defense lawyers. In other words, some defendants might have prosecution barred, others not, based on the same event. Such inconsistency does nothing to promote trust and confidence in the fairness of the process.

VIII

This I Believe

NPR HAS, IN the past, run a segment called "This I Believe" in which persons express their views on a particular subject, their values and principles, i.e., what they believe. On occasion, I have asked participants in Perception of Justice courses to do a similar exercise regarding justice, to write a short "I believe" essay that summarizes their individual code of conduct, the core principles and values which guide their behavior, and their expectations for the conduct of others.

If they wish to share their essay with the class, so much the better, but we don't require them to. The thought is that the exercise of organizing their thoughts and writing them down is helpful in itself. It helps them recognize the shape of the lens through which they view things, what affects their determination of what is fair and just in a given situation.

And I'd like you, the reader, to do that now. It doesn't have to be in final form. Indeed, you should always be open to looking at things differently if you receive new information. But you know what you think about the principles and values that guide your conduct and what you expect of others. You know what you think is fair or just. Write it down. It will help you analyze how and why you see some things as fair, or unfair, and how you balance competing principles and values. You need not share it with anyone—though I'd be pleased to receive a copy, even anonymously. There is no required form or content. So, go ahead, take some time and write your "This I Believe" essay. I'll wait.

Okay, some of you didn't write anything down, did you? Maybe you thought the request was just a rhetorical device. Maybe you just didn't want to take the time. No matter. You don't have to, of course—though I think you'd find it helpful. For those of you who hesitated, looking perhaps for an example to go by, below is what I penned many years ago. Looking at it again now, it still reflects my views. Maybe that's a good thing. Maybe not. But I thought it a good place to end our discussion on justice.

I believe in liberty and its consequential counterpart, personal responsibility, as cornerstones for any society that wants to be bound by the rule of law. Our laws and public policies should be aimed at providing and protecting as much individual freedom as is reasonably practical when living with other persons who may not always share your views. Because we almost always have the freedom to choose, we should be responsible for our choices. No excuses.

I believe in respect for everyone as a starting point.

I believe in the dignity of all work.

I believe that a perception of fairness is a fundamental foundation for any civilized society and the closer law comes to matching this general sense of justice the better.

I believe in the Golden Rule.

I believe that, in general, more laws mean less justice as well as less freedom. Stick to the fundamentals. Moreover, an unjust or unfair law, one that a large number of people do not respect, weakens the system of justice. We should prioritize and not waste time and effort promulgating, and trying to enforce, laws with which a large segment of the population disagrees.

I believe that tolerance is an important glue for society. We should tolerate others' ideas and conduct as much as possible consistent with the moral sphere (i.e., the fundamental moral values and principles that unite us.)

I believe in honesty and integrity. You should always deal in good faith with others, from honest and pure motives, never with intent to harm or take advantage of another. Your word should be your bond. If you agree to do something, you do it. If you can't for some reason, you do your best to make it right. On the flip side, if someone has tried to comply with their obligations but has been unable to do so, to the extent you can, you should release them from the obligation or at least minimize your loss.

I believe that on some issues, on which a significant number of people strongly disagree and conflict cannot be avoided by compromise, and you cannot find common ground to resolve the dispute, then you have to resolve the dispute by judicial or political decision (i.e., by a lawsuit or by a vote). These situations should be avoided as much as possible because it tears at the fabric of a society bound together by shared principles and values.

One of those shared principles and values is that the majority makes the rules and sometimes we have to accept what we don't like for the good of the community and try to change it through legitimate means. If people feel so strongly that they are not willing to abide by the accepted rules for dispute resolution, they should disobey openly, non-violently, and be willing to accept the consequences.

I believe that even if we might never know for sure what the right or ethical way is, even if we can't always achieve justice in every situation, we can and should always strive for it. To paraphrase Carl Schurz: ideals are like the stars for sailors; we may not be able to reach them, but we chart our course by them.

I would call this exercise the basis for governing by principle and principled government. If we can agree on important values and principles and apply them across the board in evaluating the words and actions of our leaders, perhaps we can begin to bridge the political divide in the country. And when I say across the board, I mean the principles and values must be applied to "our guy" just as they apply to "their guy."

Although we have focused on the judicial branch, I believe many of the principles above also apply to the other branches and to any evaluation of government action, or inaction. I also think the other branches, and the people, would do well to adopt some judicial precepts in making decisions, e.g., evidence-based decisions, made in the open, with information presented by witnesses who are under oath, subject to perjury charges. A closer look at specific issues confronting us might be interesting and helpful, but I'll leave that for another day.

As I ended my career as a judge, I was still learning and still loving my job. I could have gone on, but I was also looking forward to "the next chapter" as the cliché goes. I decided I would do nothing that could be described as gainful employment for at least a year. I would spend more time with the grandkids, travel a bit, and write more, including a book on justice. After a few false starts and many, many revisions, this volume is the result. I hope it has given you something to think about on the subject of justice.

About the Author

Terry Lewis was a trial judge from 1989 to 2019, presiding over a variety of civil and criminal cases. He is now a private attorney specializing in arbitration and mediation. He lives in Tallahassee with his wife, Fran, and their Border Collie Mix, Pepper.

terrylewisbooks.com
www.the-justice-institute.org